BRILLIANT BRAIN TEASERS

BRILLIANT BRAIN TEASERS

Exercises to Keep Your Mind Sharp

Ian Livingstone and Jamie Thomson

Skyhorse Publishing

Skyhorse Publishing books may be purchased in bulk at
special discounts for sales promotion, corporate gifts, fund-raising,
or educational purposes. Special editions can also be
created to specifications.

For details, contact the Special Sales Department, Skyhorse
Publishing, 307 West 36th Street, 11th Floor, New York, NY 10018
or info@skyhorsepublishing.com.

Skyhorse® and Skyhorse Publishing® are registered trademarks of
Skyhorse Publishing, Inc.®, a Delaware corporation.

www.skyhorsepublishing.com

10 9 8 7 6 5 4 3 2 1

Library of Congress Cataloging-in-Publication Data is available on file.

Cover design by David Ter-Avanesyan
Cover art: head © Kiyoshi Takahase Segundo;
speech bubble © Shutterstock

ISBN: 978-1-5107-7583-1

Printed in China

Contents

How to Play

Playing couldn't be easier! All you need is a pen, some paper (or you can use the blank pages provided at the back of this book), and a watch (some mobile phones have a stopwatch in them too).

Each of the fiendishly difficult puzzles in this book is numbered, but not like the pages or chapters you'd find in an ordinary book. When you've finished a puzzle, you'll be asked to turn to another numbered section in the book for the answer, and then on again for the next nasty conundrum. Sometimes you'll be asked to choose between different puzzles. This means you can replay *Brilliant Brain Teasers*, choose some different puzzles the second time around, and see if your brain has gotten bigger, so to speak! You'll often get a choice of doing a regular puzzle or a TOUGH puzzle. Tougher puzzles score more points, but can be pretty hard, so take them on only if you think your brain is pretty big in the first place, or if you're ready for them after cutting your brain teeth on some regular puzzles.

And you're not allowed to use a calculator. That's cheating and you won't get an accurate reading of your brain size if you do!

Turn over for some quick tips.

Quick Tips

Write down your solution and time taken before turning
to the answer section.

If you need to take a break for some strange reason
(such as eating, sleeping, or going to work), just note
down the section number you were at, so you can return
to it once you've got those unimportant chores
out of the way.

The puzzles are a real mix of brain-teasing conundrums—
some have several possible solutions, for some you'll need
to think a bit laterally, for others there are little clues in
the text that'll give you a hint.

TOUGH puzzles are marked with skull and crossbones.

Above all, speed is of the essence! The faster you can
solve it, the more points you'll score. But don't sacrifice
accuracy for speed. There's no point doing it fast but
getting it wrong and scoring nothing at all. You wouldn't
want to find out your brain was the size of a pea, now,
would you?

Don't worry too much if you can't solve a puzzle—there's
plenty more to score on. Do worry if it happens a lot,
though …

Scoring

Keep a running total of your score in the box provided at the back of this book, or on a scrap piece of paper. You might also need to record certain section numbers as you go along. Nearly all the puzzles are timed, and you should score yourself according to the following:

Scoring (regular puzzle)
5 minutes or less   = 2 points
More than 5 minutes = 1 point
Nothing if you don't get it right, obviously

Scoring (TOUGH puzzle)
5 minutes or less   = 4 points
More than 5 minutes = 2 points
Nothing if you don't get it right, obviously

However, give yourself *10* minutes for SPIDOKU puzzles (see later). For those puzzles where you have to give more than one answer, score yourself as above for *each* answer. This score table is also provided at the back of the book on page 266 for easy reference. When you've finished the book, compare your score to the Table of Results on page 234 and find out how big your brain is! Now all you have to do is to turn to section 1 on the next page and start reading. Good luck!

1

Welcome to *Brilliant Brain Teasers*. You'll be trying to solve a sequence of puzzles for which you will be scored. The resulting total will determine how big your brain is, and how well you use it. The puzzles will tend to get harder and harder as you progress further.

But we'll start with a few easy puzzles to get your brain ticking. Now get ready to time yourself, and turn to section **13**.

2

Remember, Remember III

This is a memory test puzzle—instead of scoring points according to how long the puzzle took, you score points for memorizing as many items as you can.

You will have two minutes to memorize the words on the page, and when the time is up you will be asked to turn to another section to give your answers. Time yourself for another two minutes and try to get down on paper as many words as you can recall. Turn to **408**.

3

Kids

Start the clock!

At a children's party, 10 kids had juice, 8 kids had cake, and 6 kids had juice and cake. How many kids were there at the party?

When you have the answer, or the time is up, turn to 112.

4

Hard Times

Start the clock!

Flynn has fallen on hard times, turned to drink and ended up a homeless tramp on the streets. He collects cigarette butts and uses the tobacco to roll his own cigarettes. For every 8 cigarette butts he finds, he rolls 1 full cigarette for himself. He has just collected 64 cigarette ends. How many cigarettes can he make?

When you think you have an answer, turn to 192.

5

The Cork and Bottle

Start the clock!

A bottle costs a dollar more than a cork. Together they cost 110 cents. How much does the bottle cost and how much does the cork cost?

When you think you have the answer, record your time and turn to **57**.

Da Glyph Code

Check out the panel of glyphs below. It's a kind of Sudoku, but the numbers are represented by symbols.

You must work out what the three numbers at the bottom of the panel are, so you have to work out what numbers the glyphs represent first. Each row and column adds up to a number, shown as a glyph at the end of each row or column.

Start the clock!

When you think you have the answer, turn to the section the three numbers represent. If you are right, it will start with the words: 'Well done, you solved Da Glyph Code!' If it doesn't start with those words, or if you can't work out the answer, turn to **274** for the next puzzle.

Answer to 394:

The Colonel was the *mother* of the Private.

When you've finished scoring, turn to **227**.

Answer to 49:

60 miles per hour. The speed of the conductor is actually irrelevant—you only need to know the time elapsed and the distance traveled.

When you've finished scoring, turn to **83** for another train-themed puzzle, or to **327** for a TOUGH puzzle.

Answer to 390:

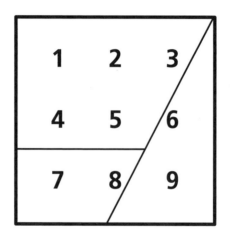

When you've finished scoring, turn to **229**.

Odd One Out III

Start the clock!

Which is the odd one out of these symbols?

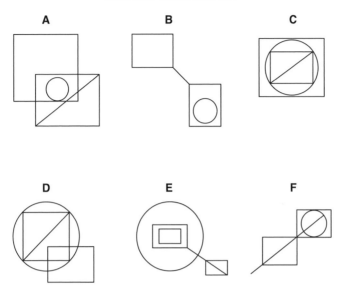

When you think you've worked it out, turn to **315**. Only 10 percent of the book left to go!

11

Bird Long 1

Start the clock!

A bird has a head 9 cm long. The tail is equal to the size of the head plus a half of the size of the body. The body is the size of the head plus the tail.

How long is the bird?

When you think you have the answer, turn to **74**.

12

Crossnumber II

Fill the blank squares with a number, using only the digits
1 to 9. Horizontal lines should add up to the totals in the
right-hand column, and vertical lines should add up to the
totals in the bottom row. There are also two diagonal
lines. One runs down from the top left-hand corner to the
bottom right-hand corner, and the other runs down from
the top right-hand corner. These should add up to 21 and
20 as shown. Good luck!

Start the clock!

				20
			7	30
	1			11
			4	20
		3		17
21	12	26	19	21

When you're finished, turn to **421**.

13

Half Full, Half Empty

Start the clock!

There are six glasses in a row. The first three are full of wine, the last three are empty. By moving only one glass, how can you set them up so that full and empty glasses are lined up alternately?

When you think you have the answer, or time runs out, turn to **33**.

14

Spidoku VI

Each of the eight segments of the spiderweb should be filled with a different number from 1 to 8, in such a way that every ring also contains a different number from 1 to 8. Some numbers are already in place. Can you fill in the rest?

Start the clock!

When you're done, or you've run out of time, turn to **355**.

15

Answers to 305:

387 + 627 = 1,014   219 x 15 = 3,285

49 x 49 = 2,401   266 – 193 = 73

3,165 – 1,895 = 1,270   798 + 647 = 1,445

12 x 13 = 156   17 x 23 = 391

11 x 394 = 4,334   6,439 – 1,587 = 4,852

365 + 153 = 518   972 – 489 = 483

4,852 – 632 = 4,220   942 x 9 = 8,478

382 x 5 = 1,910   1,201 x 5 = 6,005

Score yourself using the TOUGH score table. When you're done, turn to **372** for a regular puzzle—the first Shapes and Codes challenge.

16

Light Speed

Start the clock!

The distance from the Earth to the Sun is about 100 million miles. The speed of light is 186,000 miles per second, and light takes eight minutes to reach the Earth from the Sun. Let's say that the Sun rose at 6 am this morning, and that by some freak of physics the speed of light is suddenly doubled to 372,000 miles a second. What time will the Sun rise tomorrow?

When you think you have the answer, turn to **336**.

Hieroglyphs

Start the clock!

Look at these digital hieroglyphs, reflect on them a little, and then work out what the sixteen-digit number sequence is.

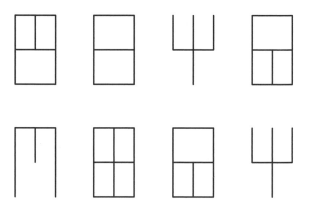

When you're ready, turn to **46**.

Speedy Math III

Time for some more speedy math.

Answer these problems as quickly as you can and write down the answers.

Start the clock!

5 + 9 =	28 – 12 =
4 x 13 =	19 + 22 =
35 – 19 =	87 + 25 =
14 x 11 =	42 + 176 =
16 x 16 =	194 – 83 =
479 + 237 =	759 – 525 =
5,671 – 1,642 =	488 + 2,187 =
12 x 423 =	

When you're done, turn to **138** for the answers and your score.

19

Ducats and Doubloons II

Start the clock!

If 6 doubloons are worth 1½ ducats, how many ducats are 27 doubloons worth?

When you think you have the answer, or you run out of time, turn to **113**.

The Banquet

Start the clock!

A great banquet was prepared for a Roman emperor and his courtiers. 22 Dormice, 40 Larks' Tongues, 30 Flamingos and 40 Roast Parrots were served. How many portions of Boiled Ostrich were served?

When you think you have the answer, or time has run out, turn to **62**. You have now completed 95 percent of the book!

21

Beauty Parlor

Start the clock!

Two beauticians have three customers, each needing a facial and a manicure. Each hairdresser takes fifteen minutes for a facial, and five minutes for a manicure. What's the quickest they can get the job done?

When you have the answer, or the time is up, turn to **185**.

22

Number Series IV

Start the clock!

What is the next number in the series?

7,645, 5,764, 4,576, ?

When you think you have the answer, turn to **262**.

Jumbled Equation III

The following equations have had their numbers jumbled. Rearrange them so they make sense. Mathematical signs remain where they are.

Start the clock!

$$(5 \times 3) + 1 = 21$$
$$(2 \times 4) + 1 = 34$$
$$(6 \times 31) + 9 = 54$$

When you think you have the answers, turn to **163**.

24

Answer to 227:

Black has the largest area, and light blue has the smallest area.

When you've finished scoring, turn to **48**.

25

Answers to 184:

68 + 23 = 91   43 – 17 = 26

15 x 9 = 135   17 + 28 = 45

98 – 47 = 51   367 + 314 = 681

13 x 13 = 169   69 + 885 = 954

27 x 14 = 378   385 – 165 = 220

599 + 264 = 863   953 – 824 = 129

7,935 – 686 = 7,249   578 + 5,473 = 6,051

55 x 27 = 1,485

When you've finished scoring, turn to **255**.

26

Spot the Difference I

Start the clock!

Here is a picture of Sinbad on a flying carpet with a bag of booty. How many differences are there between the pictures?

When you think you have the answer, or when the time limit is up, turn to **91**.

27

Hunting

Start the clock!

Two fathers and two sons, who were all poachers, went out hunting for rabbits. They bagged three in total, but they each took one home for supper. How is this possible?

When you think you have the answer, or the time is up, turn to **134**.

28

Sheep II

Start the clock!

Imagine that sheep pen again with a bunch of sheep, some of which are ewes. The number of sheep heads multiplied by the number of sheep hooves multiplied by the number of ewes' tongues equals 100. How many sheep are there, and how many of them are ewes?

When you're ready, turn to **314**.

29

Answer to 257:

The answer is 3. Any set of four adjacent numbers (i.e. any given square made up of four numbers) adds up to 14.

Score yourself using the TOUGH score table, then turn to **292**.

30

Quick Questions I

Answer these questions as quickly as you can and write down the answers.

Start the clock!

How many 4-cent sweets are there in a dozen?

How many grooves are there in an old-style 45 rpm record?

If five thousand, five hundred and three dollars is written as $5,503, how would fifteen thousand, fifteen hundred and fifteen dollars be written?

If it takes four rat catchers four minutes to kill four rats, how many rat catchers would be needed to catch 50 rats in 50 minutes?

How come 2001 dollar coins are worth more than 1999 dollar coins?

When you've written down the answers, or time has run out, turn to **252**.

31

Dark Lord's Ransom

Start the clock!

A Dark Lord ransomed two captive hobbits he didn't need anymore for 210 gold pieces. On one of them he made a profit of 10 percent on the cost he paid the bandits to kidnap him, and on the other he made a loss of 10 percent. Overall he made a profit of 5 percent. How much did he pay the bandits for each hobbit in the first place?

When you think you have an answer, turn to **267**.

32

What's Next? V

Start the clock!

What's next in this series?

O, T, T, F, F, S, S, E, N, T, E, T, T, F, F, ?

When you have the answer, or the time is up, turn to **152**.

33

Answer to 13:

Simply empty the contents of the second glass into the fifth glass.

Score yourself according to the time taken. You should be using the score table for regular puzzles (you will be told clearly when it's a TOUGH puzzle). And at the level of these starting puzzles, you should be scoring maximum points! Now turn to **66**.

34

Answers to 361:

875 + 345 = 1,220   842 x 17 = 14,314

51 x 51 = 2,601   567 – 414 = 153

6,434 – 2,543 = 3,891   64,313 + 53,421 = 117,734

19 x 18 = 342   14 x 37 = 518

11 x 738 = 8,118   78,492 – 3,521 = 74,971

3,745 + 5,468 = 9,213   864 – 389 = 475

6,548 – 2,989 = 3,559   913 x 9 = 8,217

267 x 13 = 3,471

Score yourself using the TOUGH score table, then turn to **255**.

35

Answer to 195:

It's impossible—the first lap has already taken two minutes.

When you've finished scoring, turn to **285** for a regular puzzle, or to **367** for a TOUGH Speedy Word Sum.

36

Answer to 372:

The answer is e—AY. The first part of the code refers to the top-left shape and the second to the top-right shape.

When you've finished scoring, turn to **52** for a new type of Sudoku puzzle.

37

Answer to 94:

There were 21 men in the King's bodyguard.

When you've finished scoring, turn to **239** for another Bodyguard question, or to **146** for a TOUGH Bodyguard question.

38

Answer to 374:

12. All the rows and columns add up to 24.

When you have finished scoring, turn to **222** for another Missing Number puzzle, or to **397** for a TOUGH Missing Number puzzle.

Answer to 318:

Like so!

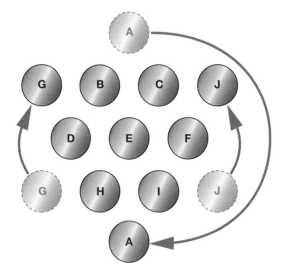

When you've scored yourself, turn **127** for a regular puzzle, or to **103** for a TOUGH puzzle.

Answer to 190:

96 cm. The head is 12 cm. The tail is 24 + 12 = 36 cm. The body is 12 + 24 + 12 = 48 cm. 12 + 48 + 36 = 96 cm.

When you've scored yourself, turn to **10**.

41

Answer to 260:

As the agent with the green badge has spoken to Agent Red, we know that Agent Red doesn't have a green badge. We already know he doesn't have a red badge. Therefore he has a yellow badge. The agent with the green badge cannot be Agent Red, nor can he be Agent Green, therefore he is Agent Yellow. So Agent Yellow has a Green badge, and Agent Red has a yellow badge, meaning Agent Green must have a red badge.

When you've finished scoring, turn to **364** for a more traditional type of puzzle.

42

Answer to 253:

Nine birds and thirteen bees. (Remember, bees have six legs!)

When you've finished scoring, turn to **11**.

43

Answer to 363:

19. It's actually two series running alternately. Add 3 to the first number, 3 to the third number, 3 to the fifth number,

etc., and subtract 3 from the second number, subtract 3 from the fourth number and so on. Nasty, eh? Or maybe not. . . .

Score yourself using the TOUGH score table, then turn to **234**.

44

Answer to 366:

16 + 32 = 48, then add 9 = 57

You might have been able to come up with a different solution than the one given here. If so, that's fine, score yourself normally. When you've finished scoring, turn to **79** for another regular CryptoMath puzzle, or to **156** for a TOUGH CryptoMath puzzle.

45

Answers to 107:

1	+	3	+	5	x	7	÷	9	=	7
1	+	3	x	5	x	7	–	9	=	131
1	+	3	x	5	–	7	+	9	=	22

You might have managed to solve this by another combination of symbols—if so, that's fine. Score yourself using the TOUGH score table, then turn to **224**.

46

Answer to 17:

The numbers are mirror images of themselves. The answer is **99 33 44 66 77 88 66 44.**

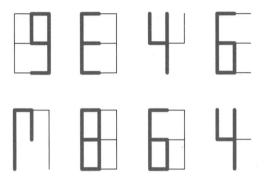

When you've finished scoring, turn to **220.**

47

Construction Conundrum

Start the clock!

The world's tallest skyscraper took seven years to build. Each year the workmen were able to double its height. How many years did it take for the skyscraper to reach half of its maximum height?

When you think you have the answer, or when the time is up, turn to **412.**

48

Remember, Remember I

This is a memory test puzzle, and it's a bit different from the others. Instead of scoring points according to how long the puzzle took, you score points for memorizing as many items as you can within the time limit.

You will have two minutes to memorize the words on the page, and when the time is up you will be asked to turn to another section to give your answers. You must then time yourself for another two minutes and try to get down on paper as many words as you can recall. Now turn to **89**.

49

Train Times I

Start the clock!

A train leaves May Station exactly on time. The train conductor leaves the driver's cab and walks the length of the train, checking tickets. It takes him half an hour to walk it, at an average speed of 1 mile per hour.
He then heads back to the driver's cab at the same speed. When he arrived back at the driver, the train was pulling into James Street Station, which is 60 miles from May. How fast was the train moving?

When you're ready, turn to **8** for the answer.

Doodlebugs

Start the clock!

Here's a row of doodles. What comes next? Choose from the numbered doodles below.

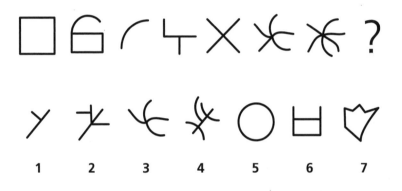

When you think you have the answer, turn to **284**.

51

Answer to 349:

Eleven minutes—you don't need to make twelve cuts. When you've finished scoring, turn to **160**.

52

Spidoku I

Each of the eight segments of the spiderweb should be filled with a different number from 1 to 8, in such a way that every ring also contains a different number from 1 to 8. The segments run from the outside of the spiderweb to the center, and the rings run all the way around. So that you can see the rings more clearly, we've shaded them gray and white. Some numbers are already in place. Can you fill in the rest?

Start the clock!

When you're done, or you've run out of time, turn to **73**.

More Missing Numbers I

Start the clock!

What number is next?

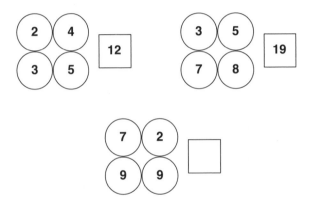

When you think you have the answer, or you have run out of time, turn to **245**.

Answers to 177:

1: Snake—the rest are mammals.
2: Orange—it's the only fruit.
3: Smile—the rest are senses.

4: Train—it's the only one that travels on rails.

5: Bat—it's the only non-feathered flyer in the group.

6: Handbag—the rest are all worn rather than carried.

7: Steel—the others occur naturally, but steel must be made.

8: Sieve—the only one that can't hold any liquid.

9: Dolphin—the only mammal.

10: Tomato—it is in fact the only fruit in the list.

When you have finished scoring, turn to **116** for another Similarities puzzle.

55

Answer to 319:

32. Each number is simply its position on the grid defined by row and column, but counting from the right. So 45 is column 4 counting from the right, and row 5, counting from the bottom.

When you've finished scoring, turn to **84** for a regular puzzle, or to **119** for a TOUGH puzzle.

56

Magic Triangle

Start the clock!

You have six numbers: 3, 5, 7, 9, 11 and 13. You must place

them in the triangle in such a way that the three numbers on each side add up to 25.

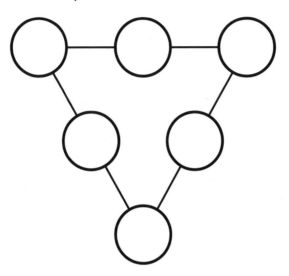

When you think you have the answer, turn to **338**.

57

Answer to 5:

The right answer is that the bottle costs 105 cents, and the cork costs 5 cents. Score yourself according to the score table.

Now turn to **26**.

58

Odd One Out IV

Start the clock!

Which is the odd one out of these symbols?

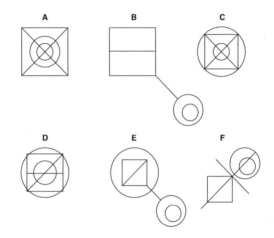

When you think you've worked it out, turn to **278**.

59

Ducats and Doubloons I

Start the clock!

If 3 doubloons are worth 2 ducats, how many ducats are 27 doubloons worth?

When you think you have the answer, or you run out of time, turn to **125**.

60

Answer to 407:

The Dark Lord started with 84 gold pieces in his Strongbox.

When you have finished scoring, turn to **86**.

61

Cut a Cross

Start the clock!

Using only four straight cuts, how can you divide this cross into five pieces that can be rearranged into a square?

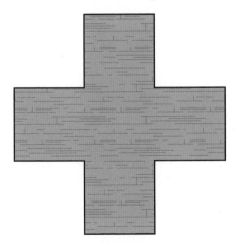

When you think you have the answer, turn to **77**.

62

Answer to 20:

42. Each vowel is worth 2 and each consonant 4, so Dormice gives 22, etc.

After scoring yourself using the TOUGH score table, turn to **206** for a regular puzzle, or to **257** for a TOUGH puzzle.

63

Answer to 238:

B is the correct cube.

When you've scored your points, turn to **251**.

64

Spidoku III

Each of the eight segments of the spiderweb should be filled with a different number from 1 to 8, in such a way that every ring also contains a different number from 1 to 8. Some numbers are already in place. Can you fill in the rest?

Start the clock!

When you're done, or you've run out of time, turn to **90**.

What's Next? VI

Start the clock!

You haven't got a prayer of doing this one! What's next in this series?

G, E, L, N, ?

When you have the answer, or the time is up, turn to **111**.

66

Start the clock!

How much does a bottle of wine weigh if it is 1 kilogram plus half its own weight?

When you think you have an answer, record your time and turn to **93**.

67

Answer to 285:

4	1	3	2	5
5	4	1	3	2
2	3	4	5	1
3	5	2	1	4
1	2	5	4	3

When you've finished scoring, turn to **308**.

A Wizards' Spat Over a Hat

The Savants of the Spectrum are a secret society of Wizards. There are four Archmages who rule the Council of Mages: the Red Wizard, the Yellow Wizard, the Blue Wizard, and the Green Wizard. They're always plotting against each other.

Each Wizard always wears a colored Wizard's hat, but no Wizard wears a hat the same color as his own name.

One day, the Yellow Wizard and the Blue Wizard got together to plot how to cast a spell banishing the other two Wizards into the Outer Darkness of Absolute Despair and General Nastiness. Rather than refer to the other Wizards by name, in case someone was listening they used the hats they were wearing as substitutes.

"So, we'll cast my red hat into the Darkness first," said the Blue Wizard.

"No, mine first!" said the Yellow Wizard.

Suddenly, the Red and Green Wizards burst into the room.

"You expect us to believe you're going to cast a spell on your own hat!" cried the Wizard with the blue hat.

"It's us you're really talking about, isn't it!" added the Green Wizard.

It wasn't long before they fell to blows . . .

Anyway, what color is each Wizard's hat?

Start the clock!

When you have an answer, turn to **281**.

When you have an answer, turn to **281**.

69

Write down on a piece of paper as many of the things from 221 as you can remember. You have two minutes to do this.

When the time is up, turn to **204**.

70

Answer to 409:

Small = ½ a liter, medium = 1 liter, large = 4 liters, or you could have small = ⅝ of a liter, medium = 1¼ liters, large = 2¾ liters.

After scoring, turn to **5** for a slightly tricky puzzle.

Speedy Unpleasant Divisions I

Answer these math problems as quickly as you can.

Start the clock!

$12 \div 4 =$	$28 \div 7 =$
$72 \div 9 =$	$1{,}365 \div 21 =$
$117 \div 9 =$	$280 \div 35 =$
$114 \div 19 =$	$1{,}736 \div 56 =$

When you're done, record the time it took you, and turn to **414** for the answers and your score.

Answer to 399:

TTTTTT, or six tails in a row.

Score yourself using the TOUGH score table. When you're done, turn to **27**.

73

Answer to 52:

Score yourself normally. Now you have a choice: if you want to do another regular Spidoku puzzle, turn to **105**. If you want to try a TOUGH Spidoku puzzle, turn to **132**.

74

Answer to 11:

72 cm. The head is 9 cm. The tail is 18 + 9 = 27 cm. The body is 9 + 18 + 9 = 36 cm. 9 + 27 + 36 = 72 cm.

When you're done scoring, turn to **190** for another bird-themed regular puzzle, or to **380** for a TOUGH puzzle.

75

Answer to 103:

Whitehaven is 40 miles away—4 miles for every letter in the town's name.

Score yourself using the TOUGH score table, then turn to **205**.

76

Answers to 360:

1: True
If Voibles are Varbles and no Varbles are Vibbles, then no Voibles can be Vibbles. A Vibble couldn't be a Voible because a Voible is a Varble, and no Varbles are Vibbles.

2: False
Look at it this way: if some dogs are animals, and all cats are animals, then some dogs are definitely cats.

3: False
There's no stated relationship between Nabobs and Nebubs, so there's no way of knowing.

4: True
Trimps = Tromps. Tromps = Trumps. Therefore Trimps = Tromps.

Score your points (if any) and turn to **359** for a slightly tricky one!

77

Answer to 61:

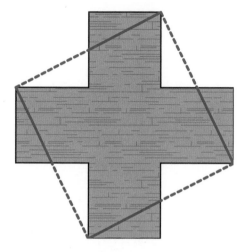

Cut as shown in the drawing. The triangles cut from each arm of the cross will fit into the gaps in between the arms. When you've finished scoring, turn to **377** for a slightly tricky question.

78

Write down on a piece of paper as many of the things from section 233 as you can remember. You have two minutes to do this. When the time is up, turn to **128**.

79

CryptoMath II

Work out what numbers each asterisk represents. Only the numbers 1 through 9 are used, and no number is used twice (including the answer).

Start the clock!

** — * = **, then minus ** = 16

When you think you've solved it, turn to **269**.

80

Quick Questions II

Answer these questions as quickly as you can, and write down the answers.

Start the clock!

Mr. and Mrs. Flynn have five sons. Each son has one sister. How many are there in the Flynn family?

A street has 100 houses, numbered 1 to 100. How many houses have the number 9 in their address?

Indiana Flynn acquired an ancient Egyptian mask for $400. He sold it for $600. Later he bought it back for $800 and then sold it again for $1000. How much profit did he make?

Dr. Flynn was on a dig in the jungles of Mexico looking for Aztec ruins. He felt something in his pocket that had a head and a tail but no legs. Didn't seem to bother him though—why was that?

When you've written down the answers, or time has run out, turn to **330**.

When you've written down the answers, or time has run out, turn to **330**.

81

Answer to 277:

The only way to do it is to put the pens inside each other, like so:

If you got it right, well done! Have you considered a career as an evil Dark Lord? Score yourself using the TOUGH score table, then turn to **209**.

82

Answer to 295:

Robin could hit the 19 twice, the 22 once and the bullseye, 40, once. Or he could hit the 13 once, the 19 twice, the 22 once, and finally the 27 once. It's possible there's yet another solution to the ones given. Score yourself normally if you manage to find one. Now turn to **368**.

83

Train Times II

Start the clock!

The train leaves May Station right on time again. The train conductor leaves from the driver's cab and walks the length of the train checking tickets. It takes him half an hour to walk it, at an average speed of 1 mile per hour. He then heads back to the driver's cab, but in a bit of a hurry, at 2 miles per hour. When he arrived back at the driver, the train was pulling into James Street Station, which is 60 miles from May. How fast was the train moving?

When you're ready, turn to **142** for the answer.

84

Box Puzzle II

Start the clock!

Which box has been opened up?

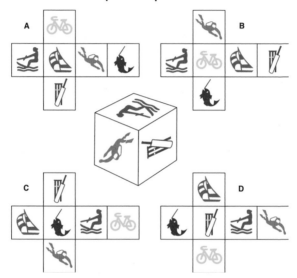

When you think you have the answer, turn to **365**.

85

Answers to 335:

Three times twelve minus five = 31

Seven times three plus fifteen minus four = 32

One hundred and five minus twenty-eight = 77

Seventy-eight plus one hundred and fourteen = 192

Seven plus ninety-five times three = 306

Fifty-three times eighteen = 954

Seventeen plus thirty-four minus five times eight = 368

Nine times ninety-three plus twenty-seven = 864

Thirty-eight plus one hundred and seventeen minus twelve = 143

One hundred and fifteen times three = 345

When you've finished scoring, turn to **110** for another regular Speedy Word Sum or to **244** for a TOUGH Speedy Word Sum.

86

Sign of the Times I

What mathematical symbols do you have to insert in between the numbers to get the correct result? Note that only the symbols +, −, x and ÷ are used.

Start the clock!

2   4   6   8   =   20

2   4   6   8   =   28

2   4   6   8   =   6

When you think you have the answers, turn to **130**.

87

Answer to 178:

TTTH

Score some points if you got it right. When you're done, turn to **393** for a regular puzzle, or to **210** for a TOUGH Heads in Your Head puzzle.

88

Answer to 359:

Mike was a greyhound . . . or a horse, a camel, a car—as long as you understand he wasn't human.

When you've finished scoring, turn to **96** for a regular puzzle or to **416** for a TOUGH puzzle.

89

You have two minutes to memorize as many of these words as you can.

Start the clock!

Green	Rock	Blue	Grass
Tobacco	Toad	Wall	Milk

Sandy	Peach	Silk	Fish
Hedgehog	Atomic	Beam	Dog
Faerie	Boxer	Unicorn	Plug

When the time is up, turn to **121**.

Answer to 64:

Score yourself normally. Now you have a choice—if you want to do another regular Spidoku puzzle, turn to **201**. If you want to try a TOUGH Spidoku puzzle, turn to **323**.

91

Answer to 26:

There are six differences.

When you've finished scoring, turn to **175**.

92

Answer to 224:

Number 6 clown did a hand stand so that they could form the number 798, which is divisible by 7.

When you've finished scoring, turn to **306**.

93

Answer to 66:

The answer is 2 kilograms. Score yourself accordingly.

Turn to 114.

94

The King's Bodyguard I

Start the clock!

King Charles had a bodyguard of knights. Two-thirds of his bodyguard were Knights of St. George, two-sevenths of them were Templar Knights and the last bodyguard wasn't a knight at all. How many men were in King Charles's bodyguard?

When you think you have the answer, turn to 37.

Music of the Hemispheres
Listening to Mozart is said to improve brain function, but tests have also shown that taking music lessons actually boosts your IQ. Learning how to read music and all that challenging music theory stuff exercises the brain to no end!

95

Weigh Anchor

Start the clock!

How many teacups are needed to balance the anchor?

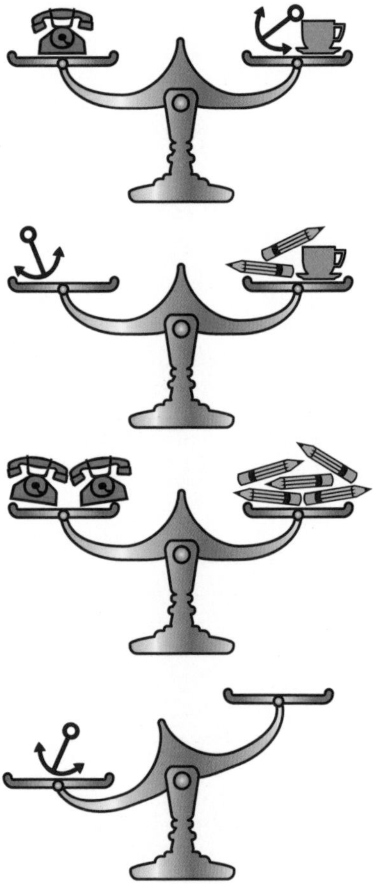

When you're done, or you've run out of time, turn to **272**.

96

Sunrise

Start the clock!

Where in the world could you see the sunrise twice in any 24-hour period?

When you have the answer, or the time is up, turn to **413**.

97

Answers to 419:

18 + 43 = 61

3 x 9 = 27

4 x 11 = 44

You may be able to get viable answers with different combinations—if so that's fine; score yourself normally. When you've finished scoring, turn to **299**.

98

Answer to 306:

1 in 24 is the correct answer—or 1 in (4 x 3 x 2 x 1). If you got it right, well done, you know your probability theory! Turn to **324**.

99

Knotted or Not II

Start the clock!

If you pulled both ends of the rope below would it end up with a knot?

When you think you have an answer, turn to **362**.

100

Stringing Along

Start the clock!

Imagine a piece of string. Now cut it at any point. You end up with a piece of string with two ends. How is this possible?

When you have the answer, or the time is up, turn to **258**.

101

Answers to 244:

Ninety-eight thousand three hundred and seven plus nine hundred and ninety-eight thousand seven hundred and five = 1,097,012

Four hundred and fifty-two thousand and five plus one hundred and eighteen thousand one hundred, plus ninety-eight = 570,203

Four million six hundred thousand and eighty-three minus two million two hundred and thirty thousand and four = 2,370,079

Thirteen hundred thousand four hundred and fifty-eight plus eighty-three thousand two hundred and sixty-four, minus twelve thousand = 201,722

Nine million nine hundred and ninety thousand nine hundred and nineteen plus five million five hundred thousand and fifty-five = 15,490,974

Remember, you have to get them *all* correct to score. Score yourself using the TOUGH score table, then turn to **390**.

102

Answer to 289:

7 + 2 = 9, then times 6 = 54, then divide by 3 = 18

You might have been able to come up with a different solution than the one given here. If so, that's fine. Score yourself using the TOUGH score table, then turn to **195**.

103

Dark Lord's Journey I

Start the clock!

A Dark Lord is leading his army of Goblin marauders deep into the territory of the White Wizard. Dawn is on its way though, and his Goblin Raiders can't stand sunlight, so he has to move quickly. He really wants to burn down the town of Whitehaven, but doesn't know how far away it is. If his base, Doomtowers, is 40 miles away, Gobton 24 miles away, Sunvale 28 miles away and Wizardskeep 44 miles away, how far is Whitehaven?

When you think you have the answer, turn to **75**.

104

Sign of the Times III

What arithmetic symbols do you have to insert in between the numbers to get the correct result? Note that only the symbols +, −, x and ÷ are used.

Start the clock!

2   4   6   8   =   44

2   4   6   8   =   16

2   4   6   8   =   9

When you think you have the answers, turn to **164**.

Improving Your IQ
It was once thought that your IQ was pretty much fixed, but tests show that it can be improved. Working memory is also important—you use your working memory when you're solving puzzles like those in this book. Brain scans of those exercising their working memories showed growth in brain activity. Brain training can also improve your IQ, by as much as 8 percent according to one study. So challenge that brain and make it grow! Physical exercise, too, is very beneficial for the brain, and some tests show that it can actually help you to grow more brain cells.

105

Spidoku II

Each of the eight segments of the spiderweb should be filled with a different number from 1 to 8, in such a way that every ring also contains a different number from 1 to 8. Some numbers are already in place. Can you fill in the rest?

Start the clock!

When you're done, or you've run out of time, turn to **147**.

106

Answers to 406:

$2 \times 4 = 8$

$4 \times 3 = 12$

$5 \times 8 = 40$

$3 \times 16 = 48$

Turn to **213** for another Jumbled Equation, or to **23** for a TOUGH Jumbled Equation.

☠107☠

Sign of the Times IV

What arithmetic symbols do you have to insert in between the numbers to get the correct result? Note that only the symbols +, –, x and ÷ are used.

Start the clock!

1	3	5	7	9	=	7
1	3	5	7	9	=	131
1	3	5	7	9	=	22

When you think you have the answers, turn to **45**.

Sheep II

Start the clock!

Imagine that sheep pen again with a bunch of sheep, some of which are ewes. The number of sheep heads multiplied by the number of sheep hooves multiplied by the number of ewes' tongues equals 588. How many sheep are there, and how many of them are ewes?

When you're ready, turn to **310** for the answer.

109

Birds and Bees I

Start the clock!

In my garden, I've got a small aviary and an apiary with only a few bees in it. There are a total of 28 eyes and 64 legs. How many birds and bees are there in my garden?

When you're ready, turn to **373** for the answer.

110

Speedy Word Problems II

Answer these math problems as quickly as you can. Remember, you have to get them all correct to score any points.

Start the clock!

Four times eight minus three =

Six times five plus twelve minus five =

One hundred fifty-two minus sixty-one =

Eighty-seven plus two hundred and thirty-one =

Eight plus sixty-four times three =

Forty-nine times fifteen =

Nineteen plus thirty-four minus eight times five =

Eleven times forty-four plus twenty-seven =

Seventy-three plus ninety-eight minus nineteen =

One hundred and twenty-eight times four =

When you're ready, record the time taken and turn to **170**.

111

Answer to 65:

D. They're the first five books of the Old Testament, the Pentateuch—Genesis, Exodus, Leviticus, Numbers and then Deuteronomy.

Score yourself using the TOUGH score table, then turn to **16**.

112

Answer to 3:

Twelve kids. Six kids had juice and cake, leaving two out of the cake eaters that didn't have juice. As there were ten juicers, there must be twelve kids in total.

When you've finished scoring, turn to **180** for a slightly tricky question.

113

Answer to 19:

6¾ ducats (27/6 = 4½. 4½ x 1½ = 6¾)

When you've finished scoring, turn to **187**.

114

Knotted or Not I

Start the clock!

If you pulled both ends of the snake below would it end up with a knot?

When you think you have the answer, record your time and turn to **139**.

115

Chests within Chests

Start the clock!

A wizard has a set of magical chests. The largest Treasure Chest has six more Treasure Chests inside it. Inside each of those there are four more. How many chests does he have in total?

When you're ready for an answer, turn to **183**.

116

Similarities II

Start the clock!

Which one of the five is least like the other four?

1: Pen—Ink—Pencil—Paintbrush—Ballpoint

2: Cauliflower—Courgette—Carrot—Fennel—Potato

3: Knee—Arm—Hair—Head—Foot

4: Ship—Plane—Helicopter—Hang-glider—Balloon

5: Eagle—Falcon—Vulture—Hawk—Cormorant

6: Bricks—Roof—Window—Chimney—Wall

7: Carbon—Nitrogen—Oxygen—Sulphur—Tin

8: Knife—Fork—Spoon—Spatula—Saucepan

9: Whale—Dolphin—Seal—Shark—Porpoise

10: Mushroom—Chicken—Carrot—Beef—Potato

Write down your answers, and when you're ready, turn to
165.

117

Answers to 215:

1: True
2: True
3: False
4: False

Score your points and turn to **30** for your next puzzle.

118

The Gambler

Start the clock!

Wild Bill had played three hands of Poker in the Saloon, each time losing three-quarters of his money. He was left with $1.50. How much has he lost in total?

When you think you have an answer, turn to **214**.

Death in the Desert

Start the clock!

The explorer, "combat archaeologist" and looter of tombs, Dr. Flynn, was trekking across the desert in search of King Solomon's Mines. Unfortunately for him, the water container in the back of his Land Rover had started leaking. In the first hour, it lost half the number of liters it held plus one liter. In the second hour, it lost half of the remainder plus one liter. In the third hour, it lost half of the remainder again, plus one liter more. In the fourth hour, it lost half the remainder plus one liter more. Now it was completely empty. How many liters did the container hold to start with?

When you think you have the answer, turn to **279**.

120

Crossnumber I

Fill the blank squares with a number, using only the digits 1 to 9 (you can use each digit more than once). Horizontal lines should add up to the totals in the right-hand column, and vertical lines should add up to the totals in the bottom row. There are also two diagonal lines. One runs down from the top left-hand corner to the bottom right-hand corner, and the other runs down from the top right-hand corner. Each of these should add up to 25 as shown. Note that you can use the same number more than once in any row or column. Good luck!

Start the clock!

				25
	2			16
			4	21
		9		21
2				10
12	19	19	20	25

When you're finished, turn to **302**.

121

Write down on a piece of paper as many of the words from 89 as you can remember. You have two minutes to do this. When the time is up, turn to **143**.

Answers to 367:

Ninety thousand four hundred and forty-three plus eighteen hundred and seventeen times three hundred and twenty-two = 29,707,720

One million three hundred and twenty-seven thousand plus two million four hundred thousand and eighteen = 3,727,018

Two hundred and fifty-five thousand and seventeen minus sixty-seven thousand and twenty-two plus one hundred and eighteen thousand = 305,995

Two hundred and twelve thousand five hundred and eighty-two plus nine thousand three hundred and four minus one hundred and four thousand three hundred and eight = 117,578

Two million nine hundred thousand nine hundred and ninety-two plus one hundred and ninety-five thousand and nineteen minus four hundred and eighty-two thousand one hundred and five = 2,613,906

Score yourself using the TOUGH score table and when you're done, turn to **308**.

123

Answers to 153:

$6 \div 2 = 3$

$63 \div 9 = 7$

$248 \div 8 = 31$

$169 \div 13 = 13$

$18 \div 6 = 3$

$156 \div 26 = 6$

$135 \div 9 = 15$

$1,365 \div 21 = 65$

Score yourself using the TOUGH score table, then turn to **216**.

124

Answer to 377:

The same number—twelve rungs. As the tide rises, so does the ship, floating on top of the water!

When you've finished scoring, turn to **366**.

125

Answer to 59:

18 ducats.

When you've finished scoring, turn to **19**.

126

Answer to 308:

The man in the photograph is the friend's son.

When you've finished scoring, turn to **266**.

127

Only One II

Start the clock!

Only one of these objects appears in both drawings.
Can you find it?

When you think you have the answer, turn to **263**.

128

Answers to 233:

Here's a list of all the pictures:

Plane, Fish, Bus, Umbrella,

Key, Ambulance, Tree, Bird,

Musical notes, Guitar, Envelope, Happy face,

Train, Palm tree, Candle, Skull and crossbones.

Score yourself half a point for every one you remembered (they don't have to be word perfect. For instance, if you wrote down "coach" and we had it as a "bus" that's fine, you still score).

When you've finished scoring, turn to **349** for a regular puzzle, or to **221** for a TOUGH memory puzzle.

129

Answer to 291:

T for Twenty-nine. They're all prime numbers, starting with the first, 2, 3, 5, 7, 11, 13, 17, 19, 23 and then 29.

Score yourself using the TOUGH score table, then turn to **3**.

130

Answers to 86:

$$2 + 4 + 6 + 8 = 20$$

$$2 + 4 \times 6 - 8 = 28$$

$$2 \times 4 \times 6 \div 8 = 6$$

You might have managed to solve this by another combination of symbols—if so, that's fine, score yourself normally. When you've finished scoring, turn to **215** for a regular puzzle, or to **331** for another Sign of the Times puzzle, but this time a TOUGH one.

131

Write down on a piece of paper as many of the words from 191 as you can remember. You have two minutes to do this. When the time is up, turn to **217**.

☠132☠

Spidoku II

Each of the eight segments of the spiderweb should be filled with a different number from 1 to 8, in such a way that every ring also contains a different number from

1 to 8. Some numbers are already in place. Can you fill in the rest?

Start the clock!

When you're done, or you've run out of time, turn to **168**.

133

Answer to 293:

None—the plough being pulled along behind the ox erases all the tracks. This was actually a trick question found on an ancient Babylonian clay tablet!

When you've finished scoring, turn to **335**.

134

Answer to 27:

There were three poachers, a grandfather, a father and his son.

When you've finished scoring, turn to **179** for a regular puzzle, or to **95** for a TOUGH puzzle.

135

Answer to 202:

8:24 PM. The second clock ran for 7 hours and 20 minutes, putting on 1½ minutes every hour, or 11 minutes, so the real time when it stopped was 7:09 PM. And it stopped 1 hour and 15 minutes ago, so the first clock now shows 8:24 PM.

After you have finished scoring, turn to **32**.

136

Answer to 225:

B and E are the same.

When you've finished scoring, turn to **21**.

137

Answer to 386:

The precise answer is 98 seconds. Her hair *always* grows at 50 cm a second, all the way.

If your answer was 99, 100, or 101 seconds, score yourself normally. However, if you got it bang on as 98 seconds, give yourself an additional 2 bonus points on top of your normal score! Now turn to **161** for one last TOUGH puzzle.

138

Answers to 18:

$5 + 9 = 14$	$28 - 12 = 16$
$4 \times 13 = 52$	$19 + 22 = 41$
$35 - 19 = 16$	$87 + 25 = 112$
$14 \times 11 = 154$	$42 + 176 = 218$
$16 \times 16 = 256$	$194 - 83 = 111$
$479 + 237 = 716$	$759 - 525 = 234$
$5,671 - 1,642 = 4,029$	$488 + 2,187 = 2,675$
$12 \times 423 = 5,076$	

When you've finished scoring, you can turn to **184** for more Speedy Math or to **361** for TOUGH Speedy Math.

139

Answer to 114:

Yes.

When you've finished scoring, turn to **154**.

140

Answer to 393:

Neither—the egg yolk is yellow!

When you've finished scoring, turn to **115**.

141

Answer to 299:

E. All the symbols have two lines, one square, and one circle, except for E, which only has one line.

When you've scored your points, turn to **417** for a regular puzzle, or to **71** for a TOUGH puzzle.

142

Answer to 83:

80 miles per hour. This time, the speed of the conductor is

relevant, as you need to know it in order to work out the time elapsed, enabling you to work out the train's speed.

When you've finished scoring, turn to **22**.

143

Answers to 89:

Here are the words again:

Green	Rock	Blue	Grass
Tobacco	Toad	Wall	Milk
Sandy	Peach	Silk	Fish
Hedgehog	Atomic	Beam	Dog
Faerie	Boxer	Unicorn	Plug

Score yourself half a point for every word you got right.

Next is another memory test. Turn to **182** for another regular one, or turn to **193** for a TOUGH memory test.

144

Answer to 197:

21 squares.

When you've finished scoring, turn to **396** for a regular puzzle, or to **289** for a TOUGH puzzle.

145

Answer to 205:

D. It's the first letters of some of the months of the year beginning with March.

When you've finished scoring, turn to **181** for another series puzzle, or to **291** for a TOUGH series puzzle.

The King's Bodyguard II

Start the clock!

One-third of King Charles's bodyguard were Knights of St. George, a fifth of them were Templar Knights and three times the difference between those two numbers were Boogie Knights, and the last bodyguard wasn't actually a knight at all. How many men were in King Charles's bodyguard?

When you think you have the answer, turn to **402**.

Brain fact: The average adult human brain weighs 1,360 grams.

Brain fact: On average, there are 100 billion neurons in the human brain.

147

Answer to 105:

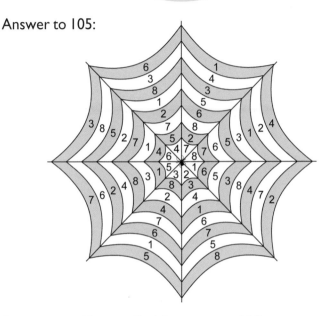

Score yourself normally. Now turn to **189**.

148

Heads

Start the clock!

There are five head of cattle in a paddock. A rancher enters the paddock and leaves with two heads. How many are left in the paddock?

When you have the answer, or the time is up, turn to **287**.

149

Answer to 368:

127. The series is simple—double the number and add one.

When you've scored yourself, turn to **316** for another Number Series puzzle, or to **363** for a TOUGH Number Series puzzle.

150

Answer to 323:

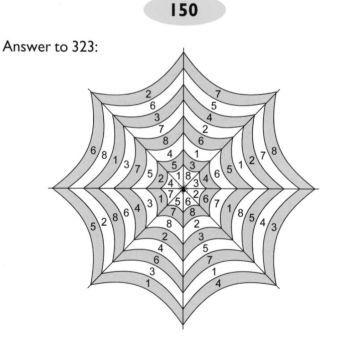

Score yourself using the TOUGH score table. Now turn to **80**.

151

Answer to 229:

The blue circle in column 2, row 4 is the right one to push! If you got it wrong, you score nothing, and poor old Dr. Flynn dies a horrible death!

When you've finished scoring, turn to **350**.

152

Answer to 32:

S. It's simply the first letters of the numbers One, Two, Three, Four, etc.

When you've finished scoring, turn to **270** for another regular What's Next? puzzle, or to **65** for a TOUGH What's Next? puzzle.

Brain fact: Although the brain accounts for only 2 percent of the whole body's mass, it uses 20 percent of all the oxygen we breathe. A continuous supply of oxygen is necessary for survival. A loss of oxygen for 10 minutes can result in significant neural damage.

Brain fact: About 750 milliliters of blood pumps through your brain every minute!

Speedy Unpleasant Divisions II

Answer these math problems as quickly as you can—note that you'll need to get them all correct to score any points.

Start the clock!

$6 \div 2 =$ $18 \div 6 =$

$63 \div 9 =$ $156 \div 26 =$

$248 \div 8 =$ $135 \div 9 =$

$169 \div 13 =$ $1{,}365 \div 21 =$

When you're done, turn to **123**.

154

Something Doesn't Add Up

Start the clock!

When can you add two to eleven and get one as the answer?

When you think you've got the answer, record your time and turn to **173**.

155

Weighty Matters II

Start the clock!

A set of scales is in balance. On one side is a gold ingot, on the other side, half an ingot and a ¾ kilogram weight. How heavy is a gold ingot?

When you think you have the answer, or when the time is up, turn to **172**.

🕱156🕱

CryptoMath II

Work out what numbers each asterisk represents. Only the numbers 0 to 9 are used, and no number is used twice (including the answer). Don't forget that zero!

Start the clock!

* x ** + * + * = **, then add * = 93

When you think you've solved it, turn to **370**.

157

Weighty Matters I

Start the clock!

A set of scales is in balance. On one side are 3½ bags of rice, on the other, 1¾ bags of rice and a ¼ kilogram weight. How heavy is a bag of rice?

When you think you have the answer, or when the time is up, turn to **334**.

158

Answers to 213:

$3 \times 16 = 48$

$4 \times 8 = 32$

$5 \times 12 = 60$

When you've finished scoring, turn to **376**.

159

Answer to 288:

HHH

Score your points, if you got it right. The next one is another coin puzzle like this one. You can either turn to **188** for a regular one, or to **399** for a TOUGH one.

Spidoku V

Each of the eight segments of the spiderweb should be filled with a different number from 1 to 8, in such a way that every ring also contains a different number from 1 to 8. Some numbers are already in place. Can you fill in the rest?

Start the clock!

When you're done, or you've run out of time, turn to **300**.

More Missing Numbers II

Start the clock!

This is the last puzzle! What number is next?

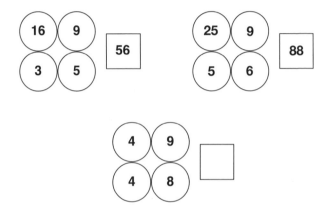

When you think you have the answer, or you have run out of time, turn to **391**.

Building Pyramids

Start the clock!

The Mayans are building one of their step pyramids out of cubic stone blocks. The pyramid is going to have eleven steps up to the summit, and each step is one block deep and one block high. The uppermost level of the pyramid is ten by ten blocks squared. How many blocks will be needed to build the whole structure?

Remember, no calculator cheating, but on the plus side, you only need an approximate answer.

When the time is up, or you think you have the answer, turn to **333**.

163

Answers to 23:

$(3 \times 2) + 5 = 11$

$(4 \times 3) + 2 = 14$

$(5 \times 13) + 4 = 69$

Score yourself using the TOUGH score table, then turn to **376**.

164

Answers to 104:

$2 + 4 \times 6 + 8 = 44$

$2 \times 4 - 6 \times 8 = 16$

$2 + 4 \div 6 + 8 = 9$

You might have managed to solve this by another combination of symbols—if so, that's fine, score yourself normally. When you've finished scoring, turn to **357** for a regular puzzle, or to **107** for a TOUGH Sign of the Times puzzle.

165

Answers to 116:

1: Ink—the rest are writing implements.

2: Fennel—it's the only one also used as flavoring (the seeds).

3: Hair—the rest are living body parts; hair is actually "dead."

4: Ship—the only one on sea, rather than in the air.

5: Vulture—the only bird that eats carrion.

6: Bricks—the only thing everything else could be made of.

7: Tin—it's the only metal in the list.

8: Saucepan—the only one that's a container.

9: Shark—the rest have blowholes.

10: Mushroom—it's the only fungus, the rest are either meat or vegetable.

When you've finished scoring, turn to **275**.

166

Answer to 209:

Eleven Evil Geniuses. Five Galactic Overlords had Virgin's Blood and Anti-heroes Delight, leaving two out of the Supervillains that didn't have Virgin's Blood. As there were nine Dark Lords, there must be eleven Evil Geniuses in total.

When you've finished scoring turn to **64** for some more Spidoku!

167

Answer to 376:

There are 26 Jersey cows and 76 Guernsey cows.

When you have scored, turn to **286** for a regular puzzle, or to **420** for a TOUGH puzzle.

Mental Act
It's possible for the brain to keep track of several things at once, as proved by a man in southern India who performed a magnificent mental juggling act. While playing a chess game (without seeing the board), he learned a poem, answered general knowledge questions, kept count of how many times a bell was rung, memorized two lines of Spanish, and did mental arithmetic calculations.

168

Answer to 132:

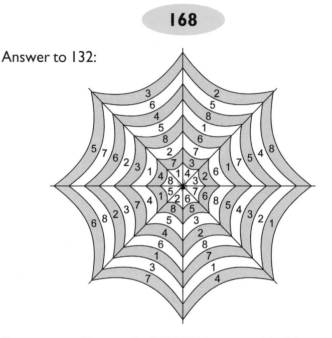

Score yourself using the TOUGH score table. Now turn to **189**.

169

When Number Series Go Wrong II

Start the clock!

Which one of these numbers doesn't belong in the series?

2, 8, 4, 16, 8, 24, 32, 16, 64, 32

When you think you have the answer, turn to **259**.

170

Answers to 110:

Four times eight minus three = 29
Six times five plus twelve minus five = 37
One hundred fifty-two minus sixty-one = 91
Eighty-seven plus two hundred and thirty-one = 318
Eight plus sixty-four times three = 216
Forty-nine times fifteen = 735
Nineteen plus thirty-four minus eight times five = 225
Eleven times forty-four plus twenty-seven = 511
Seventy-three plus ninety-eight minus nineteen = 152
One hundred and twenty-eight times four = 512

When you're done, turn to **390**.

171

Answers to 339:

Dragon Guardian: 150 gold pieces
Hell-hound Wrangler: 700 gold pieces
Magician Architect: 600 gold pieces
Orc Overseer: 400 gold pieces
Master of Slaves: 1,500 gold pieces
Conjuror of the Demon Hordes: 1,800 gold pieces

When you have finished scoring, turn to **326**.

172

Answer to 155:

1½ kilograms.

When you've finished scoring, turn to **386**.

173

Answer to 154:

When you add two hours to eleven o'clock, you get one o'clock!

Score yourself. Now we're going to start with some new kinds of puzzles. Things will start heating up! Turn to **203**.

Jumbled Equation V

The following equations have had their numbers jumbled. Rearrange them so they make sense. Mathematical signs remain where they are.

Start the clock!

$$5 \times 1 \div 120 = 6$$

$$12 \div 45 \times 6 = 8$$

$$222 + 15 \times 6 - 3 = 9$$

When you think you have answers, turn to **271**.

175

Missing Number 1

Start the clock!

Can you work out what the missing number should be?

12		32			
				54	
	25		?		

When you are ready, or out of time, turn to **218**.

176

Answer to 396:

12 squares and 24 triangles.

When you've finished scoring, turn to **195**.

177

Similarities I

Start the clock!

Which one of the five is least like the other four?

1: Lion—Bull—Cat—Snake—Horse

2: Bean—Orange—Corn—Pea—Carrot

3: See—Hear—Touch—Smile—Smell

4: Motorbike—Car—Truck—Tractor—Train

5: Bat—Robin—Nightingale—Eagle—Falcon

6: Shoes—Blouse—Handbag—Hat—Skirt

7: Steel—Iron—Lead—Copper—Tin

8: Bowl—Sieve—Plate—Jug—Saucepan

9: Dolphin—Shark—Sailfish—Tuna—Barracuda

10: Turnip—Tomato—Marrow—Onion—Potato

Write down your answers, and when you're ready, turn to **54**.

178

Heads in Your Head III

Remember, you're not allowed to use real coins!

Start the clock!

Imagine four coins in a row, all tails up.

Now turn the two middle coins over.

Now turn the far right-hand coin over.

Now move the inside coins to the outside.

Now move the second coin in from the left out to the left-hand edge of the row.

Now turn both the inner coins over.

What have you got left?

When you think you have the answer, turn to **87**.

Brain fact: There is no sense of pain within the brain itself. This fact allows neurosurgeons to probe areas of the brain while the patient is awake. Feedback from the patient during these probes is useful for identifying important regions, such as those for speech.

179

Lone Wolf II

Start the clock!

Which object appears once only?

When you think you have an answer, turn to **345**.

180

Kings and Beards

Start the clock!

Doc Flynn was playing poker in the saloon using an ordinary pack of playing cards. Wild Bill suddenly spoke up: "If two out of the four Kings have beards, how many beards do all the Kings in the deck have?"

When you have the answer, or the time is up, turn to **348**.

181

What's Next? IV

Start the clock!

What's next in this series?

R, O, Y, G, B, I, ?

When you have the answer, or the time is up, turn to **404**.

182

Remember, Remember II

Start the clock!

You have two minutes to memorize as many of these words as you can:

Sword	Ratchet	Fork	Pocket
Pink	Saucepan	Pillar	Wine
Leaf	Candle	White	Noodle
Gammon	Tire	Fridge	Banana
Pedal	Thimble	Cloak	Beard

When the time is up, turn to **256**.

183

Answer to 115:

31 (1 + 6 + 24)

When you've finished scoring, turn to **197** for a regular puzzle, or to **232** for a TOUGH memory puzzle.

184

Speedy Math IV

Do this math as quickly as you can and write the answers down.

Start the clock!

68 + 23 =	43 – 17 =
15 x 9 =	17 + 28 =
98 – 47 =	367 + 314 =
13 x 13 =	69 + 885 =
27 x 14 =	385 – 165 =
599 + 264 =	953 – 824 =
7,935 – 686 =	578 + 5,473 =
55 x 27 =	

When you're done scoring, turn to **25**.

185

Answer to 21:

Thirty minutes is the fastest—one of them does a facial and three manicures, while the other does two facials.

When you've finished scoring, turn to **358**.

186

The correct answer to 324 is none!

If you think about it, if three figures have the right head, then the fourth *must* be right too! When you've finished scoring, turn to **2**.

Brain Pie
In Tokyo in 1995, Hiroyuki Goto memorized the number pi (3.14159…) to 42,195 decimal places! This took him hours. To give you an idea of what an incredible task this must have been, here are the first 100 digits that he had to learn:

3.141592653589793238462643383279502884197169399
3751058209749445923078164062862089986280348253
421170679

187

Square Bashing

Start the clock!

How many squares of all possible sizes can you get from this diagram?

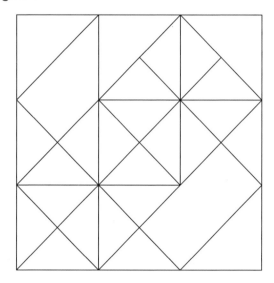

When you think you have an answer, turn to **207**.

188

Heads in Your Head II

Remember, you're not allowed to use real coins.

Start the clock!

Imagine four coins in a row, all tails up.

Now turn the far left-hand coin over.

Now turn the far right-hand coin over.

Now move the inside coins to the outside.

Now move the second coin in from the left out to the left-hand edge of the row.

Now turn both the inner coins over.

What have you got left?

When you think you have the answer, turn to **280**.

189

How Old is He?

Start the clock!

Jack O'Flynn was asked how old he was. "In two years I'll be twice as old as I was six years ago." How old is Jack?

When you think you have the answer, or the time is up, turn to **241**.

190

Bird Long II

Start the clock!

A bird has a head 12 cm long. The tail is equal to the size of the head plus a half of the size of the body. The body is the size of the head plus the tail.

How long is the bird?

When you think you have the answer, turn to **40**.

Remember, Remember IV

Start the clock!

You have two minutes to remember as many of these words as you can:

Nevertheless	When	Think	Mild
Perhaps	Was	Win	Change
Were	Am	Will	Variegated
Sideways	Typify	Indicate	Dry
Who	Note	Exchange	Florid

When the time is up, turn to **131**.

192

Answer to 4:

9. He can make 8 from the 64 he's collected, and then an additional cigarette from those 8 once he's smoked them.

When you've finished scoring, turn to **374**.

193

Remember, Remember II

Start the clock!

You have two minutes to remember as many of these words as you can:

Pastel	Idea	Feeble	Glaze
Probable	Sometimes	Never	Team
Humor	Chosen	Deep	Consular
Theology	Wednesday	However	Deplore
Ascend	Conclusion	Innovate	Side

When the time is up, turn to **356**.

Battle Drones

Start the clock!

Earth was under attack by marauding Mechanoids—robotic machine aliens from another world. Five Earth Force pilots returned from a sortie into space after destroying several Mechanoid Battle Drones. Ibrahim shot down 10 more than Juan. Luke shot down 4 less than Ibrahim. Juan and Vladimir shot down 9 between them. Vladimir shot down 2 more than Chi, but Luke shot down 3 more than Vladimir.

How many Battle Drones were shot down in all?

When you think you have the answer, or time has run out, turn to **282**.

195

Le Mans Go Carts

Start the clock!

The go-cart track is one mile long. If a driver does the first lap at 30 miles per hour, how fast must he drive to complete the second lap, so that both laps are completed in two minutes?

When you have an answer, turn to **35**.

196

Answer to 385:

Five sheep, two of which are ewes. When you've finished scoring, turn to **28** for another Sheep puzzle, or **108** for a TOUGH Sheep puzzle.

197

Dots and Squares

Start the clock!

How many squares of all possible sizes can you get from this cross of dots?

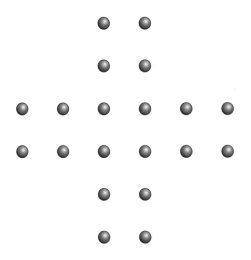

When you think you have an answer, turn to **144**.

198

How Old Is He? II

Start the clock!

Jack O'Flynn had been asked before how old he was. At the time he said: "Five years ago my Dad was five times older than me, but now he is only three times older!" How old is Jack and how old is his father?

When you think you have the answer, or the time is up, turn to **290**.

199

Answer to 341:

The can of cashew nuts is much lighter than all the others, so we know that one contains nuts and that its label is wrong. If we open one other can we will know its contents and that the label is wrong. That leaves two cans, each of which we know is wrongly labeled (i.e. it doesn't contain what the label says it does). Therefore, knowing what two other cans contain means we can work out what each of the last ones contains.

Score yourself using the TOUGH score table and turn to **11**.

Dots and Triangles

Start the clock!

How many triangles of all possible sizes can you get from this square of dots?

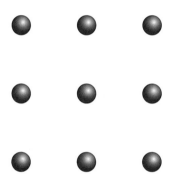

When you think you have the answer, turn to **254**.

A Full Brain?
An ordinary computer contains about 200 gigabytes of storage—room for a lot of information. However, some neuroscientists estimate that the human brain has a capacity of around 100,000 gigabytes! Another scientist has worked out that we're able to store about 2 bits of new information per second. Over a lifetime, this means we store about 1 gigabyte. Maybe this explains why our brains never get full.

201

Spidoku IV

Each of the eight segments of the spiderweb should be filled with a different number from 1 to 8, in such a way that every ring also contains a different number from 1 to 8. Some numbers are already in place. Can you fill in the rest?

When you're done, or you've run out of time, turn to **265**.

202

Clocks

Start the clock!

Two clocks were telling the right time at midday, but then the second clock began to go fast, adding 1½ minutes every hour. It stopped 1 hour and 15 minutes ago, showing a time of 7.20 pm. What time is the first clock showing now?

When you think you have the answer, or time has run out, turn to **135**.

Eating Your Way to a Better Brain
The brain consumes more calories then any other organ. It needs good food—fizzy drinks and junk food have been shown in tests to reduce the mental powers of kids. Junk and processed foods contain lots of trans-fatty acids (whatever they are!) which can slow down brain function. Tests on rats made fat by a diet of junk food rich in these acids were worse at getting out of mazes than other rats. But good carbs and fiber can boost performance. Apparently, beans on toast is a good breakfast. Also important are eggs, which boost acetylcholine, a neurotransmitter (low levels of which are said to impair brain performance). Free radicals can also retard brain power, so make sure you've got plenty of antioxidants in your diet too.

203

Speedy Math

For this test, you'll be asked to solve a series of relatively easy math problems. You just have to do them as quickly as you can! You will need to write down the answers as well, in the space provided at the back of the book or on a scrap piece of paper.

Start the clock!

$2 + 8 =$	$18 - 15 =$
$7 \times 9 =$	$15 + 18 =$
$24 - 13 =$	$25 + 67 =$
$12 \times 11 =$	$89 + 112 =$
$26 \times 13 =$	$168 - 75 =$
$387 + 122 =$	$564 - 121 =$
$8,531 - 246 =$	$568 + 1,198 =$
$231 + 450 =$	$98 + 850 =$

When you're done, record your time and turn to **249**.

204

Answers to 221:

Here's a list of all the pictures.

Clock, Moon, Motorbike, Headphones,
House, Books, Anchor, Camera,
Sofa, No-smoking sign, Pencil and clipboard, Star of David,
Key, Envelope, Glasses, Spider,
Projector, Umbrella, Stereo system, Thermometer,
Mobile phone, TV, Bicycle, Raining cloud.

Score yourself one point for every one you remembered (they don't have to be word perfect—for instance, if you wrote down "motorcycle" and we have it as a "motorbike," that's fine, you still score a point).

When you've finished scoring, turn to **160**.

205

What's Next? III

Start the clock!

What's next in this series?

M, A, M, J, J, A, S, O, N, ?

When you have the answer, or the time is up, turn to **145**.

206

Dinner by Candle Light

Start the clock!

A power outage leaves you with only candles for light. Except you've run out—all you've got left are 45 candle stubs from previous blackouts. 5 stubs will make 1 full candle, however, which will burn for half an hour. How many hours of light can you get from your candles?

When you're ready with an answer, turn to **375**.

207

Answer to 187:

18

After scoring, turn to **409**.

208

Answers to 232:

Here's a list of all the pictures:

Cat, Flag, Bomb, Cross,

Hand, Boat, Arrow, Leaf,

Teddy Bear, Five, Pirate, Cup and saucer,

Unhappy face, Star, Man, Bicycle,

Knife and fork and plate, Tent, Plane, Stag, Anchor, Sun, Police car, Flower.

Score yourself one point for every one you remembered (they don't have to be word perfect—for instance, if you wrote down "crucifix" and we had it as a "cross" that's fine, you still score a point).

When you've finished scoring, turn to **396** for a regular puzzle, or to **289** for a TOUGH puzzle.

209

Evil Geniuses

Start the clock!

At a convention of Evil Geniuses, various cocktails were drunk before a dinner of Smoked Hobbit Heart and Crushed Angel Wing Jelly. The Geniuses were variously Dark Lords, Supervillains or Galactic Overlords, some were qualified to be both Overlords and Villains, or Dark Lords and Overlords, etc., and some were all three. Kang the Merciless was the guest of honor, seen by all as the paragon of evil, for he was a Dark Lord, a Supervillain and a Galactic Overlord all rolled into one. Nine Dark Lords drank "Virgin's Blood," seven Supervillains had "Anti-heroes Delight" and five Galactic Overlords had "Virgin's Blood" and "Anti-heroes Delight." How many Evil Geniuses were there at the convention?

When you have the answer, or the time is up, turn to **166**.

Heads in Your Head IV

Remember, you're not allowed to use real coins.

Start the clock!

Imagine six coins in a row, all heads up.

Now turn over the two innermost coins.

Now exchange them with the coins next to them.

Now turn over the two outermost coins at each end.

Now take the coin next to the one on the left-hand end, and move it out to the left hand end and turn it over.

Now take the coin next to the one on the right-hand end, and move it out to the right-hand end and turn it over.

What have you left?

When you think you have the answer, turn to **343**.

211

Start the clock!

Scott of the Antarctic is in his tent. He has a gas stove, a paraffin heater, a candle, a wax taper, and only one match. Which should he light first?

When you think you have the answer, or if time runs out, turn to **351**.

212

Answer to 292:

Note that it might be possible to get a solution that's different from the one given here. If so, you still score yourself normally.

When you've finished scoring, turn to 118 for a regular puzzle or to 174 for a TOUGH puzzle.

				22
2	4	6	7	19
1	1	4	5	11
5	3	7	4	19
8	2	3	9	22
16	10	20	25	19

213

Jumbled Equation III

The following equations have had their numbers jumbled. Rearrange them so they make sense. Mathematical signs remain where they are.

Start the clock!

$$3 \times 81 = 64$$

$$8 \times 2 = 43$$

$$6 \times 20 = 15$$

When you think you have answers, turn to **158**.

214

Answer to 118:

$94.50. Working backwards, 1.50 is a quarter of 6, 6 is a quarter of 24, and 24 is a quarter of 96, which was the total number of dollars he started with.

When you've finished scoring, turn to **157**. You're getting near the end now!

215

True or False? 1

Start the clock!

Answer all four of these as fast as you can.

1: If all Bogles are Borgles and all Borgles are Beagles, then all Bogles are definitely Beagles.

2: If all Fimbles are Fombles and no Fombles are Thimbles, then no Thimbles are definitely Fimbles.

3: If some Bobalobs are Pobalobs and all Shmobalobs are Pobalobs, then some Bobalobs are definitely Shmobalobs.

4: If some Nakinaks are Niknaks and some Niknaks are Nokinoks, then some Nakinaks are definitely Nokinoks.

When you think you've got the answers (and written them down) turn to **117**.

Number Grid

Start the clock!

You have 7 digits (1, 2, 3, 4, 5, 6 and 7). You must arrange them in the grid below in such a way that no number is connected by a line to another number that's 1 greater or 1 less than that number (i. e. 2 can't be connected to 1 or 3, 6 can't be connected to 5 or 7, etc.).

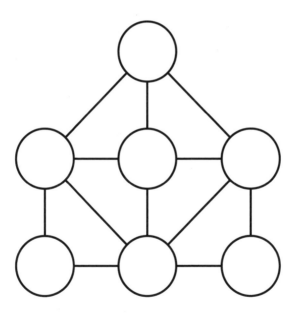

When you think you have a solution, or if time runs out, turn to **298**.

217

Answers to 191:

Here are the words again:

Nevertheless	When	Think	Mild
Perhaps	Was	Win	Change
Were	Am	Will	Variegated
Sideways	Typify	Indicate	Dry
Who	Note	Exchange	Florid

Score yourself one point for every word you remembered correctly.

When you are ready, turn to **32**.

218

Answer to 175:

45. Each number is simply its position on the grid defined by row and column, so 32 is column 3, row 2. So the answer is column 4, row 5—or 45.

When you've finished scoring, turn to **319** for another Missing Number puzzle.

219

A Full Spectrum of Puzzles

Start the clock!

Which is the next symbol in this series?

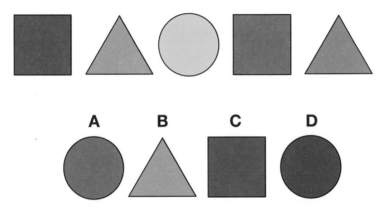

A   B   C   D

When you think you have the answer, turn to **307**.

A Knight to Remember
Master chess players have performed amazing feats of memory. In 1977 the Hungarian chess player James Flesch played 52 games of chess simultaneously while blindfolded. Unable to see any of the boards, he had to picture the position of each game in his head!

220

Rebus Puzzles I

Here are some easy Rebus puzzles to get you in the right frame of mind. What well-known word, or turn of phrase, do each of these represent?

Start the clock!

When you're ready, or the time is up, turn to **353**.

☠221☠

A Gallery of Memories III

You have two minutes to memorize the items on the page. When the time is up, turn to another section to write down as many as you can remember.

Start the clock!

When the time is up, turn to **69**.

222

Missing Number IV

Start the clock!

What's the missing number?

5	3	15
2	4	8
3	6	?

When you've finished scoring, turn to **246**.

223

Answers to 326:

Here's a list of all the pictures:

Sunglasses, Pencil, Trophy, Apple,

Earth, Flag, Present, Heart,

Ladybird, Bed, Pig, Telephone,

Clock, Dog, Eye, Scissors.

Score yourself half a point for every one you remembered

(they don't have to be word perfect—for instance, if you wrote down "globe" or "planet" and we had it as "Earth" that's fine, you still score).

When you've finished scoring, turn to **360**.

Clown Math

Start the clock!

How can the clowns arrange themselves so that their numbers show a three-digit number divisible by seven?

When you think you have an answer, turn to **92**.

225

Mondrian Madness II

Start the clock!

Which two of these Mondrian-type pictures are exactly the same?

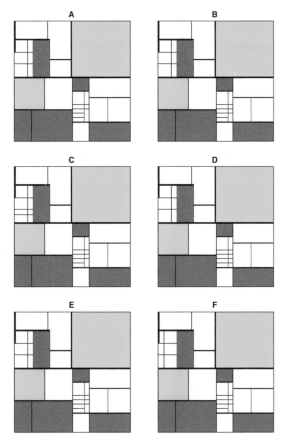

When you've got an answer, turn to **136**.

Rebus Puzzles III

Start the clock!

Try to guess the well-known phrase or word from the pictures.

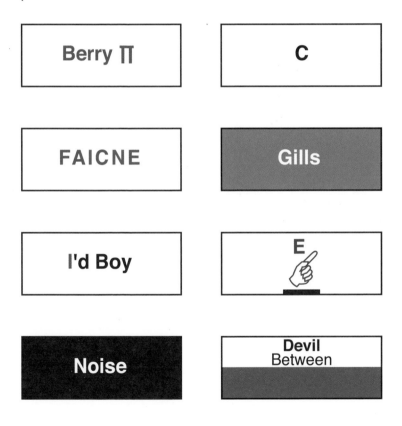

When you're ready, or you've run out of time, turn to **403**.

Area Art I

Start the clock!

Which shape has:

1. the largest area?
2. the smallest area?

(And you're not supposed to use a ruler or other device.)

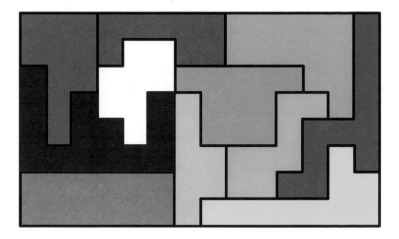

When you're ready, or out of time, turn to **24**.

228

Mondrian Madness I

Start the clock!

Which two of these Mondrian-type pictures are exactly the same?

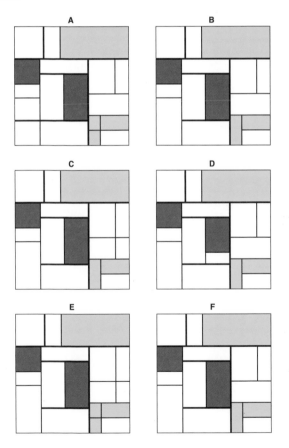

When you've got an answer, turn to **387**.

229

Key to Atlantis

Start the clock!

Dr. Flynn, combat archaeologist and plunderer of tombs, has found a grid of buttons guarding the entrance to the long lost city of Atlantis. One button will open the gates—any other button will lead to instant death! He has a clue though, written on an old piece of parchment.

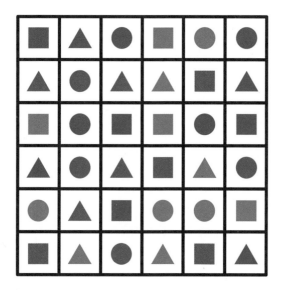

It is in a row or column with a red triangle.
It has a circle one square above it.
It is not next to a green triangle.
It is not next to a blue square.

When you have the answer, turn to 151.

230

Rebus Puzzles II

Start the clock!

Try to guess the well-known phrase or word from the pictures.

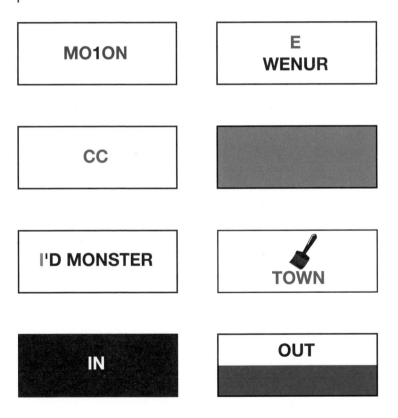

When you're ready, or you've run out of time, turn to
247.

231

Area Art II

Start the clock!

Which shape has:

1. the largest area?
2. the smallest area?

(And you're not supposed to use a ruler or other device.)

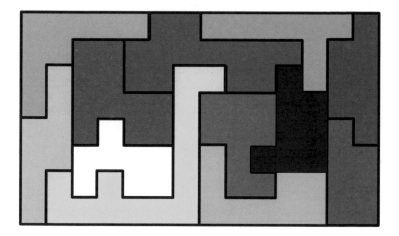

When you are ready, or out of time, turn to **250**.

A Gallery of Memories IV

You have two minutes to memorize the items on the page.
When the time is up, turn to another section to write
down as many as you can remember.

Start the clock!

When the time is up, turn to **294**.

233

A Gallery of Memories II

You have two minutes to memorize the items on the page. When the time is up, turn to another section to give your answers. You will then have another two minutes to try and write down as many items as you can remember.

Start the clock!

When the time is up, turn to **78**.

234

Comparisons

Start the clock!

Which one of the five makes the best comparison?

1: Brother is to Sister as Niece is to:
Mother—Father—Aunt—Uncle—Nephew

2: Arrow is to Bow as Shell is to
Snail—Cannon—Scorpion—Tank—Crab
3: Father is to Mother as Aunt is to:
Nephew—Niece—Uncle—Brother—Sister
4: Grapes are to Wine as Oranges are to
Cake—Marmalade—Juice—Chocolate—Ice lollies
5: Hand is to Glove as Hat is to
Hatbox—Head—Hand—Hatband—Milliner
6: Hammer is to Nail as Spanner is to
Bolt—Nut—Screw—Flange—Washer
7: Paper is to Pen as Canvas is to
Paint—Palette—Brush—Easel—Frame

Write down your answers, and when you're ready, turn
to **389**.

235

As instructed in 326, you have two minutes to memorize
as many of these pictures as you can:

When the time is up, turn to **384**.

Mondrian Madness II

Start the clock!

Which two of these Mondrian-type pictures are exactly the same?

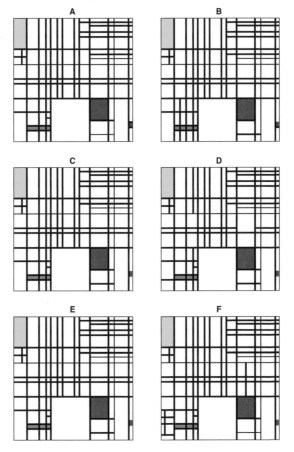

When you've got an answer, turn to **320**.

237

Answer to 274:

Two. Put three planets on each side of the scale. If they balance then one of the other three must be the one. In this case, take two of them and weigh them. If they balance, it's the other one, if they don't balance, then you also know.

If the original weighing doesn't balance, then take two from the light pile and compare their weights. If they're the same, then it's the third planet that's the light one; if they don't balance, well then it's the lighter one.

When you've finished scoring, turn to **332** for a regular puzzle, or to **53** for a TOUGH puzzle.

How Does Your Brain Work?
Your brain is about the same size and shape as two adult fists put together. It is divided into two halves, joined together by the *corpus callosum*. Although these two halves of the brain look the same, they have very different functions. Each half looks after one side of the body, but the LEFT half of your brain controls the RIGHT side of your body, while the RIGHT half of your brain controls the LEFT side of your body.

238

Box Puzzle I

Start the clock!

Which box has been opened up?

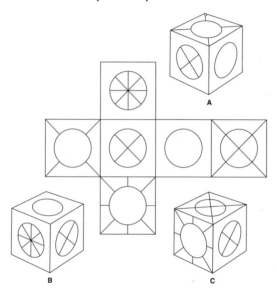

When you think you have the answer, turn to **63**.

239

The King's Bodyguard II

Start the clock!

Two-thirds of King Charles's bodyguard were Knights of St.George, two-sevenths of them were Templar Knights and the last bodyguard wasn't a knight at all. Some of the bodyguards were killed defending the King from a large band of assassins. One-seventh of the Knights of St.George were killed, and a third of his Templar Knights were killed. Each knight who died took an assassin with him, and the only bodyguard who wasn't a knight killed three on his own. The rest of the surviving knights drove off an equal number of assassins who fled the field. How many assassins were there?

When you think you have the answer, turn to **378**.

240

How Tall is He?

Start the clock!

If Mr. Flynn is 90 centimeters plus half his height, how tall is he?

When you're ready, or time has run out, turn to **325**.

241

Answer to 189:

Jack is 14.

When you've finished scoring, turn to **198**.

242

Answer to 371:

9, the first number! Starting from the 7, the series goes
n − 3, n + 2, n − 3, n + 2, etc.

Score yourself using the TOUGH score table, then turn to
148 for a regular puzzle, or to **169** for a TOUGH Number
Series puzzle.

243

Shapes and Codes II

Start the clock!

Have a careful look at the shapes and codes below. Which
code matches the shape at the end of the row?

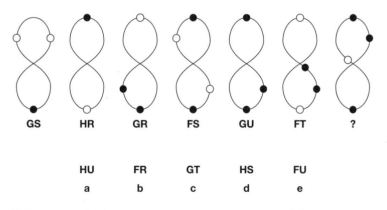

| | GS | HR | GR | FS | GU | FT | ? |

	HU	FR	GT	HS	FU
	a	b	c	d	e

When you think you have an answer, turn to **321**.

Speedy Word Problems II

Answer these problems as quickly as you can, and remember you have to get them all correct to score any points.

Start the clock!

Ninety-eight thousand three hundred and seven plus nine hundred and ninety-eight thousand seven hundred and five =

Four hundred and fifty-two thousand and five plus one hundred and eighteen thousand one hundred plus ninety-eight =

Four million six hundred thousand and eighty-three minus two million two hundred and thirty thousand and four =

Thirteen hundred thousand four hundred and fifty-eight plus eighty-three thousand two hundred and sixty-four minus twelve thousand =

Nine million nine hundred and ninety thousand nine hundred and nineteen plus five million five hundred thousand and fifty-five =

When you are ready, record your time and turn to **101**.

245

Answer to 53:

35. The two top digits are squared and then added together. You then add the two bottom digits and subtract them from the sum of the top two squared digits to get the number in the box.

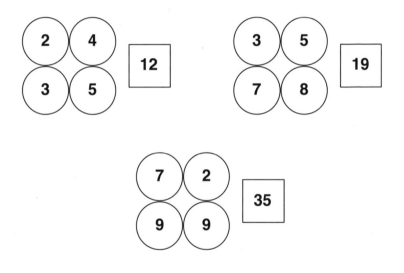

Score yourself using the TOUGH score table, then turn to **109**.

246

Answer to 222:

18. The first two numbers in the row are multiplied to give the last number in the row.

When you've finished scoring, turn to **31**.

247

Answers to 230:

Once in a Blue Moon, Ready When You Are, To See Red, Gray Area (or Greyed Out will do), Green-eyed Monster, Paint the Town Red, In the Black, Out of the Blue.

When you've finished scoring, turn to **61**.

Brain fact: Information travels at different speeds within different types of neurons. Transmission can be as slow as 0.5 meters per second or as fast as 120 meters per second. Traveling at 120 meters per second is the same as going 268 miles per hour.

Spidoku VI

Each of the eight segments of the spiderweb should be filled with a different number from 1 to 8, in such a way that every ring also contains a different number from 1 to 8. Some numbers are already in place. Can you fill in the rest?

Start the clock!

When you're done, or you've run out of time, turn to **352**.

249

Answers to 203:

2 + 8 = 10	18 – 15 = 3
7 x 9 = 63	15 + 18 = 33
24 – 13 = 11	25 + 67 = 92
12 x 11 = 132	89 + 112 = 201
26 x 13 = 338	168 – 75 = 93
387 + 122 = 509	564 – 121 = 443
8,531 – 246 = 8,285	568 + 1,198 = 1,766
231 + 450 = 681	98 + 850 = 948

When you've finished scoring, you can turn to **273** for another Speedy Sum or to **305** for a TOUGH Speedy Sum. TOUGH puzzles give you more points than regular puzzles.

250

Answer to 231:

Yellow has the largest area, and dark blue has the smallest area.

When you've finished scoring, turn to **318**.

251

Odd One Out I

Start the clock!

Which is the odd one out of these symbols?

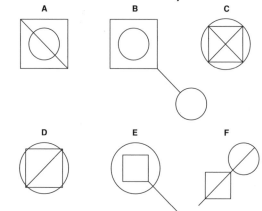

When you have an answer, turn to **346**.

252

Answers to 30:

There are a dozen sweets. Their cost is irrelevant!

There are two grooves on a record, one on each side.

$16,515

The same number of rat catchers—four.

2001 dollar coins = $2,001, which is more than $1,999!

When you've finished scoring, turn to **228**.

253

Birds and Bees II

Start the clock!

Back to my garden, where I've got that small aviary and an apiary. Today the numbers have changed. There are a total of 44 eyes and 96 legs. How many birds and bees are there in my garden?

When you're ready, turn to **42** for the answer.

254

Answer to 200:

16

When you've finished scoring, turn to **211** for a slightly tricky question.

Keep On Eating
Yogurt is a must for the brain—it provides the amino acid tyrosine, which helps in the creation of certain neurotransmitters needed for good brain function. Then there's the much talked about omega-3 fish oils, which help to lubricate the wheels of your brain. So eat lots of fish, and also strawberries and blueberries apparently. If you eat the right foods, the puzzles in this book will be a little easier!

255

Brothers and Sisters

Start the clock!

Julie says to her brother Pete: "I have as many sisters as brothers."

"Yeah, well," replies Pete: "I've got twice as many sisters as I have brothers."

How many sisters and brothers are there?

When you're ready, turn to **381** for the answer.

256

Write down on a piece of paper as many of the words from 182 as you can remember. You have two minutes to do this. When the time is up, turn to **296**.

##

Missing Number V

Start the clock!

What's the missing number in the bottom left-hand corner?

2	6	4	3	2	6
4	2	2	5	4	2
2	6	4	3	2	6
4	2	2	5	4	2
?	5	5	2	3	5

When you think you have the answer, or time has run out, turn to **29**.

258

Answer to 100:

The string was tied together to form a circle.

When you've finished scoring, turn to **200** for a regular puzzle, or to **328** for a TOUGH puzzle.

259

Answer to 169:

24. The series goes: multiply by 4, divide by 2, multiply by 4, divide by 2, etc.

Score yourself using the TOUGH score table, then turn to **20**.

260

Spies

Start the clock!

Agents Yellow, Red and Green each have a green badge, a yellow badge and a red badge, but none of them has a badge color that matches their name. They met when called to a conference at headquarters.

The Agent with the Green badge said "I have a license to kill!" to which Agent Red replied sarcastically: "What, time?"

What color is each Agent's badge? When you have an answer, turn to **41**.

261

Answer to 379:

72 miles per hour. Let's say it's 60 miles (it's not necessary to know the actual distance) to the auto shop, so it takes him an hour to get there on the first trip. Therefore it takes him 40 minutes to get home, at 90 miles per hour (or 1.5 miles per minute). So, he's traveled a total of 120 miles in 100 minutes, or an average speed of 1.2 miles per minute: 1.2 times 60 equals 72 miles per hour.

When you've finished scoring, turn to **100**.

262

Answer to 22:

6,457. The last digit is moved to the front to make the next number.

When you've scored yourself, turn to **371** for a TOUGH variant on the Number Series puzzle.

263

Answer to 127:

A beetle.

When you have finished scoring, turn to **205**.

264

Answers to 388:

8 ÷ 4 = 2	21 ÷ 7 = 3
54 ÷ 9 = 6	702 ÷ 13 = 54
112 ÷ 8 = 14	186 ÷ 31 = 6
126 ÷ 18 = 7	1,242 ÷ 23 = 54

Score yourself using the TOUGH score table, then turn to **49**.

265

Answer to 201:

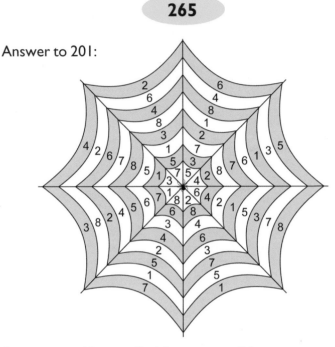

Score yourself normally. Now turn to **80**.

266

It's All Relative II

Start the clock!

A woman pointed at a picture of a man and said: "That man's mother was my mother's mother-in-law." What relationship is the woman to the man in the picture?

When you think you have an answer, turn to **418**.

267

Answer to 31:

He paid 150 gold pieces for the first hobbit and 50 gold pieces for the second. If he made a profit of 5 percent, it means he paid the bandits 200 gold pieces to kidnap the hobbits (5 percent of 200 = 10). Therefore the sum of the 10 percent loss and the 10 percent profit must add up to +10, which means the profit-making amount must be much larger than the loss-making amount. Using that as a guide, it then becomes a question of trying out a few numbers that add up to 200, one being much larger than the other, until you can find the right combination: 150 plus 10 percent = 165; 50 minus 10 percent = 45; 165 plus 45 = 210.

When you have finished scoring, turn to **379** for a regular puzzle, or to **194** for a TOUGH puzzle.

268

Answer to 350:

It's simple—he just divides each pair of numbers by 4 to get the combination code 7 3 4 8. The trick is to realize that no number can be higher than 8, as shown on the lock illustration.

When you've finished scoring, turn to **219**.

269

Answer to 79:

57 − 9 = 48, then minus 32 = 16

You might have been able to come up with a different solution than the one given here. If so, that's fine, score yourself normally. When you've finished scoring, turn to **238**.

270

What's Next? VI

Start the clock!

What's next in this series?

F, T, F, T, T, T, T, F, F, F, F, S, S, S, S, E, E, N, ?

When you have the answer, or the time is up, turn to **297**.

271

Answers to 174:

$5 \times 12 \div 6 = 10$

$8 \div 2 \times 14 = 56$

$6 + 12 \times 3 - 25 = 29$

Score yourself using the TOUGH score table, then turn to **157**. You're nearing the end now!

272

Answer to 95:

9 teacups. If 5 pencils equal 2 telephones, therefore 1 telephone equals $2\frac{1}{2}$ pencils, or to put it another way, $\frac{2}{5}$ of a telephone equals 1 pencil. Therefore $\frac{4}{5}$ of a telephone plus one teacup equal an anchor. Now, if we add a teacup to both sides of the scale, we get 1 anchor plus a teacup—a telephone in other words—equal to $\frac{4}{5}$ of a telephone plus 2 teacups. Therefore 2 teacups equal $\frac{1}{5}$ of a telephone, so 1 teacup equals $\frac{1}{10}$ of a telephone. As an anchor plus a teacup equal a telephone, then an anchor must weigh $\frac{9}{10}$ of a telephone. And as a teacup weighs $\frac{1}{10}$ of a telephone, we need 9 teacups to balance out an anchor!

Score yourself using the TOUGH score table, and when you're done, turn to **406**.

273

Speedy Math II

Do this math as quickly as you can and write the answers down.

Start the clock!

41 + 38 =	21 – 15 =
7 x 7 =	18 + 19 =
31 – 18 =	78 + 31 =
9 x 13 =	78 + 234 =
27 x 11 =	143 – 65 =
365 + 153 =	972 – 489 =
4,852 – 632 =	942 + 2,732 =
382 x 3 =	99 x 33 =

When you're ready, record your time and turn to **337**.

274

Weighing Planets

Start the clock!

A minor god, tasked with creating a solar system for the Supreme Being, was supposed to have nine planets of equal weight. Unfortunately, one of them didn't weigh as much as it should. Using a Cosmic Balance—which works just like an old-fashioned set of kitchen scales with weights and so on, only, well, bigger—what's the least number of weighings the godling could make to find the underweight planet?

When you think you have an answer, or time has run out, turn to **237**.

275

Portentous Dates

Start the clock!

What's special about July 6, 1989, specifically at 23:45 PM?

When you have the answer or the time is up, turn to **395**.

276

Answer to 358:

Lucy Gray has a yellow handbag, Hilary Yellow has a red handbag and Jane Red has a gray handbag.

Lucy Gray couldn't have a gray handbag, nor could she have a red one, as we know the lady with the red handbag made a comment. Therefore she has a yellow handbag.

The lady with the red handbag can't be Lucy Gray, nor can she be Jane Red, therefore she must be Hilary Yellow. Therefore Jane Red must have a gray handbag.

When you've finished scoring, turn to **260** for another logic puzzle, or to **68** for a TOUGH logic puzzle.

Orc Pen

An apprentice Dark Lord is just setting out on his career as an evil overlord. Unfortunately, so far he's only been able to get 21 Orcs to follow him. Not only that, they're all from different Orcish clans and keep fighting among themselves. How can he divide his square Orc pen in such a way that he's left with four pens, each pen holding an odd number of Orcs?

When you think you have the answer, turn to **81**.

Answer to 58:

E. All of the symbols have two rectangles, two lines and two circles, except for E which has three circles.

When you've scored your points, turn to **49**.

279

Answer to 119:

Thirty liters. The way to solve it is to work backwards—to get zero after the fourth hour it must have lost one plus one more. So in the third hour it must have lost half of six, plus one more to leave two and so on.

Score yourself using the TOUGH score table, then turn to **339**.

280

Answer to 188:

HHTT

Score some points if you got it right! When you're done, turn to **27**.

281

Answer to 68:

We know the Blue Wizard has a red hat. We know the Yellow Wizard can't have a yellow hat or a red hat so he has a blue or green hat. But a Wizard bursts in who has a blue hat, so the Yellow Wizard must have a green hat. The Green Wizard, who adds to a comment to the Wizard who has a blue hat, therefore can't have a blue hat, so he has a yellow hat, and the Red Wizard has a blue hat.

Score yourself using the TOUGH score table, then turn to **364** for a more traditional type of puzzle.

282

Answer to 194:

35. Ibrahim got 13, Chi got 4, Luke got 9, Vladimir got 6 and Juan got 3.

Score yourself using the TOUGH score table, then turn to **100**.

283

Answers to 303:

4 moves is the right answer! Or 16 moves in total.

Score yourself using the TOUGH score table, then turn to **386**.

284

Answer to 50:

The correct answer is D. Each doodle has a number of line endings (i. e. the square has no line endings, the second symbol has one, the third symbol two, and so on). The sequence simply goes with an extra line ending every time, so the next doodle needs seven endings, meaning the correct answer is doodle D.

When you've finished scoring, turn to **385**.

285

Logi Place

This is Sudoku with a twist. Fill the grid below so that every row, column, and shaped box contains the numbers 1–5.

Start the clock!

When you think you've finished, turn to **67**.

286

Jumbled Equation IV

The following equations have had their numbers jumbled. Rearrange them so they make sense. Mathematical signs remain where they are.

Start the clock!

$$9 \times 7 = 23$$

$$68 \times 8 = 4$$

$$2 \times 4 = 76$$

When you think you have answers, turn to **411**.

287

Answer to 148:

Four. The rancher left with one head of cattle and his own head on his shoulders.

When you've finished scoring, turn to **20** for a TOUGH puzzle.

288

Heads in Your Head I

You're not allowed to use real coins to solve this one.

Start the clock!

Imagine three coins in a row, all tails up.

Now turn the right-hand end coin over.

Now move the middle coin to the left-hand end of the row and turn it over.

Now move the middle coin to the right-hand end of the row and turn it over.

What are you left with, i. e. Head, Tail, Head (or HTH) TTT, THT, HTT, THH or HHH?

When you think you have the answer, turn to **159**.

CryptoMath III

Work out what numbers each asterisk represents. Only the numbers 1 through 9 are used, and no number is used twice (including the answer).

Start the clock!

* + * = *, then times * = **, then divide by * = 18

When you think you've solved it, turn to **102**.

290

Answer to 198:

Jack is 10 and his father is 30.

When you've finished scoring, turn to **313**.

What's Next? IV

Start the clock!

What's next in this series?

T, T, F, S, E, T, S, N, T, ?

When you have the answer, or the time is up, turn to **129**.

292

Crossnumber III

Fill the blank squares with a number, using only the digits 1 to 9. Horizontal lines should add up to the totals in the right-hand column, and vertical lines should add up to the totals in the bottom row. There are also two diagonal lines. One from the top left-hand corner runs down to the bottom right-hand corner, and the other runs down from the top right-hand corner. These should add up to 19 and 22 as shown. Good luck!

Start the clock!

				22
	4		7	19
				11
	3		4	19
				22
16	10	20	25	19

When you're finished, turn to **212**. You are nearing the end!

293

Babylonian Farmers

Start the clock!

A Babylonian ox is ploughing a field. The field is 20 feet by 20 feet, and the ox is 4 feet wide. How many tracks will it leave when it's ploughed the field?

When you think you have an answer, turn to **133**.

294

Write down on a piece of paper as many of the things from 232 as you can remember. You have two minutes to do this. When the time is up, turn to **208**.

295

Robin Hood

Start the clock!

Robin Hood is at an archery contest. If he wins, Maid Marian is released. If he loses, she will be forced to marry the evil Sheriff of Nottingham. But the Sheriff knows Robin is the best archer in the land and can always hit his target—but how good is his math?

Where must Robin shoot to score 100 points in total? (He can use as many arrows and hit each score as many times as he likes.)

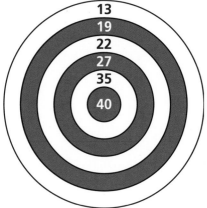

When you think you have an answer, or time has run out, turn to **82**.

Answers to 182:

Here are the words again:

Sword	Ratchet	Fork	Pocket
Pink	Saucepan	Pillar	Wine
Leaf	Candle	White	Noodle
Gammon	Tire	Fridge	Banana
Pedal	Thimble	Cloak	Beard

Score yourself half a point for every word you got right.

Now turn to **317**.

297

Answer to 270:

N for Ninety-five. It's the first letters of the numbers Five, Ten, Fifteen, Twenty, Twenty-five, Thirty, etc.

When you've finished scoring, turn to **16**.

298

Answer to 216:

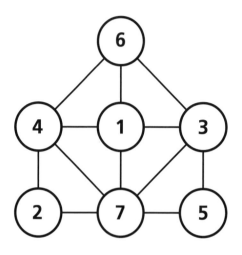

When you've finished scoring, turn to **4** for a regular puzzle, and **162** for a TOUGH puzzle.

299

Odd One Out II

Start the clock!

Which is the odd one out of these symbols?

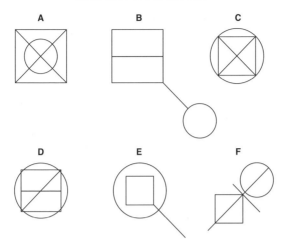

When you have an answer, turn to **141**.

Answer to 160:

Score yourself normally. Now you have a choice: if you want to do another regular Spidoku puzzle, turn to **14**. If you want to try a TOUGH Spidoku puzzle, turn to **248**.

301

Answer to 344:

Glasses.

When you've scored yourself, turn to **209**.

302

Answer to 120:

				25
5	2	1	8	16
4	6	7	4	21
1	8	9	3	21
2	3	2	5	10
12	19	19	20	25

Note that it might be possible to get a solution that's different from the one given here. If so, you still score yourself normally. When you've finished scoring, turn to **12**.

Knight Moves

Start the clock!

There are two black knights and two white knights on a three by three piece of chess board as per the illustration.

Following the rules of chess, what's the smallest number of moves *each* knight must make to put the white knights on the squares currently occupied by the black knights and vice versa?

When you think you have the answer, or you have run out of time, turn to **283**.

Jumbled Equation I

The following equations have had their numbers jumbled. Rearrange them so they make sense. Mathematical signs remain where they are.

Start the clock!

$$(5 \times 7) + 2 = 14$$
$$(1 \times 7) + 9 = 34$$
$$(1 \times 49) + 8 = 26$$

When you think you have answers, turn to **410**.

Speedy Math II

Do this math as quickly as you can and write the answers down.

Start the clock!

$387 + 627 =$	$219 \times 15 =$
$49 \times 49 =$	$266 - 193 =$
$3{,}165 - 1{,}895 =$	$798 + 647 =$

12 x 13 =	17 x 23 =
11 x 394 =	6,439 – 1,587 =
365 + 153 =	972 – 489 =
4,852 – 632 =	942 x 9 =
382 x 5 =	1,201 x 5 =

When you're done, record the time it took you, and turn to **15**.

306

Action Figures I

Start the clock!

There's a factory where an automated assembly line is putting heads on groups of four different variations of an action figure, in this case, that great gunslinger and gambler of the old west, Wild Bill. The computer is supposed to set the appropriate head on each doll, but it has just developed a malfunction. As four different action figures come along, the computer now assigns their heads randomly. What's the chance of all four figures getting the right heads?

When you think you have the answer, or if time has run out, turn to **98**.

307

Answer to 219:

D. The shapes go Square, Triangle, Circle, Square, Triangle, etc., and the colors are the colors of the rainbow—so red, orange, yellow, green, blue, indigo and then violet. So the answer is D, the indigo circle!

When you've finished scoring, turn to **344** for a regular puzzle, or to **277** for a TOUGH puzzle.

308

It's All Relative I

Start the clock!

Imagine the future, where spaceships sail the solar winds, boldly going where no man has gone before, etc. Imagine an Intergalactic Federation scout pilot returns from an eighteen-month trip (subjective time) into deep space. When he returns to Earth, twenty years have passed, because of relativity, although only six months have passed for him. He meets his oldest friend in a bar for a reunion. The old friend takes out a photograph and shows it to the pilot. "And who might this be?" says the pilot to his friend. "I don't recognize him."

"Well," says his friend: "Brothers and sisters have I none,

but this man's father is my father's son." What's the relationship between the man in the photograph and the scout pilot's friend?

When you have an answer, turn to **126**.

309

Answer to 328:

The ships are: HMS *Indomitable*, HMS *Osprey*, HMS *Revenge*, HMS *Swift*, HMS *Guardian* and HMS *Prince*.

Ship	1	2	3	4	5	6
Guns	2 guns	2 guns	1 gun	0 guns	1 gun	0 guns
Helicopter	Yes	No	Yes	Yes	Two	No
Comtower	No	Yes	Yes	No	Yes	No

Guardian			Gua	Gua	Gua	Gua
Indomitable	Ind			Ind		Ind
Prince		Pr			Pr	Pr
Revenge	Re	Re	Re	Re		Re
Swift				Sw		Sw
Osprey		Os				Os

If *Indomitable* is next to *Osprey* only 1 Ind and 2 Os fit. *Prince* cannot be 5 because she would then be next to *Swift*. Therefore she must be number 6 and Swift number 4. Then you can work out the rest.

After scoring with the TOUGH score table, turn to **229** for a slightly tricky question.

310

Answer to 108:

Seven sheep, three of which are ewes. Score yourself using the TOUGH score table, then turn to **17**.

311

Answers to 331:

1	+	3	x	5	+	7	÷	9	=	3
1	x	3	+	5	x	7	–	9	=	47
1	+	3	+	5	–	7	x	9	=	18

You might have managed to solve this by another combination of symbols—if so, that's fine. Score yourself using the TOUGH score table. When you've finished, turn to **30**.

312

Well done, you solved Da Glyph Code! Score yourself using the TOUGH score table, then turn to **274**.

313

Conjunction of the Planets

Start the clock!

Five stars in the sky are arranged in such a way that certain ancient astronomers and magicians could draw lines to create two rows of three stars, like so:

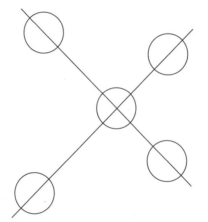

How could you add one more star so that there will be four rows with three stars in each row?

When you think you have the answer, turn to **342**.

314

Answer to 28:

Five sheep, only one of which is a ewe (5x4 = 20 hooves, so 5 x 20 x 1 = 100). When you've finished scoring, turn to **17**.

315

Answer to 10:

E. All the symbols have two rectangles, one line and one circle, except for E which has three rectangles.

When you've scored your points, turn to **58** for another regular Odd One Out or to **388** for a TOUGH puzzle.

316

Number Series II

Start the clock!

What is the next number in the series?

9, 15, 23, 33, ?

When you think you have the answer, turn to **392**.

317

Start the clock!

Take four 9s and, using as many Mathematical symbols as you like, connect them up so that they equal 100.

When you think you have the answer, or time has run out, turn to **369**.

318

Ye Olde Triangle of Coins

Start the clock!

Ten coins have been laid out in a triangle thus:

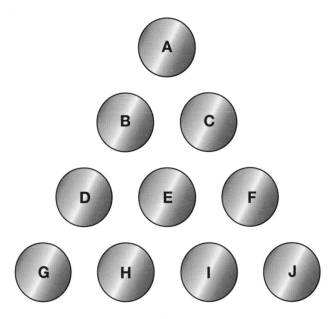

How can you make the triangle point downward by moving only three coins? You may want to sketch it out, or even lay it out with your own coins or anything else you have handy.

When you think you have the answer, turn to **39**.

319

Missing Number II

Start the clock!

Can you work out what the missing number should be?

65		45			
			23		
	52		?		

When you are ready, or out of time, turn to **55**.

320

Answer to 236:

C and E are the same.

Score yourself using the TOUGH score table, then turn to **21**.

321

Answer to 243:

The answer is b—FR.

When you've scored yourself, turn to **216**.

322

Answer to 364:

The bicycle.

When you've scored your points, turn to **99**.

☠323☠

Spidoku IV

Each of the eight segments of the spiderweb should be filled with a different number from 1 to 8, in such a way that every ring also contains a different number from 1 to 8. Can you fill in the blanks?

Start the clock!

When you're done, or you've run out of time, turn to **150**.

324

Action Figures II

Start the clock!

We're still talking about those heads. What are the chances that only three of the action figures will get the right heads?

When you think you have the answer, turn to **186**.

325

Answer to 240:

Mr. Flynn is 180 centimeters tall. When you've finished scoring, turn to **50**.

326

A Gallery of Memories I

This is a memory test puzzle, and is a bit different from the others. Instead of scoring points according to how long the puzzle took, you score points for memorizing as many items as you can within a time limit.

You will have two minutes to memorize as many of the things on the page as you can, and when the time is up, you will be asked to turn to another section to give your answers. You must then time yourself for another two minutes and try and get down on paper as many items as you can recall. Now turn to **235**.

Dark Lord's Journey II

Start the clock!

Once again, the Dark Lord was leading his army of Goblin marauders on a raid, this time into hobbit lands. "Hobbit killing—oh, what fun!" he thought to himself. His army came to a crossroads where some signs gave him a clue as to how far away the hobbits' main town was. If his base, Death Tower, is 119 miles away, Greenton is 98 miles away and Weedfarm is 75 miles, how far is Hobbit City?

When you think you have the answer, turn to **405**.

Brain fact: When you were born, your brain weighed about 350–400 grams and you had almost all the brain cells you will ever have. In fact, your brain was closer to its full adult size than any other organ in your body! Your brain stops growing when you reach 18 years.

Naval Gazing

Start the clock!

What are the names of each ship?

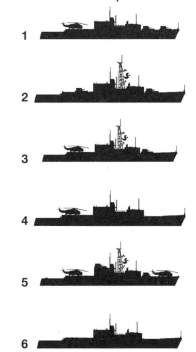

HMS *Guardian* doesn't have guns.

HMS *Indomitable* doesn't have a comtower.

HMS *Prince* either has two helicopters or none at all.

HMS *Revenge* doesn't have two helicopters.

HMS *Swift* doesn't have a gun.

HMS *Osprey* doesn't have a helicopter.

HMS *Prince* isn't next to *Swift*, but *Indomitable* is next to *Osprey*.

When you think you have an answer, turn to **309**.

329

Answers to 357:

Tin of beans = $2.40

Tin of tuna = $1.60

Tin of corned beef = $0.80

When you've finished scoring, turn to **224**.

330

Answers to 80:

Eight (five sons, one daughter, mother and father).

There are nineteen houses with 9 in their address.

Indiana made a total profit of $400.

It was a coin.

When you've finished scoring, turn to **240**.

Sign of the Times II

What mathematical symbols do you have to insert in between the numbers to get the correct result? Note that only the symbols +, −, x and ÷ are used.

Start the clock!

| 1 | 3 | 5 | 7 | 9 | = | 3 |

| 1 | 3 | 5 | 7 | 9 | = | 47 |

| 1 | 3 | 5 | 7 | 9 | = | 18 |

When you think you have the answers, turn to **311**.

Divisions

Start the clock!

If you divide 50 by a half and add 5, what is the answer?

When you are ready, or when the time is up, turn to **382**.

333

Answer to 162:

If you answered between 4,500 and 5,500 blocks, you win! If you answered 4,840 precisely, you've done very well indeed. Add 2 points to your TOUGH scoring total.

The trick is to remember each level will be two more in width than the one above it: 10 by 10 blocks equal 100. One step down, the blocks are 12 by 12, two steps down they're 14 by 14, and so on.

Now turn to **374**.

334

Answer to 157:

$\frac{1}{7}$ of a kilogram.

When you've finished scoring, turn to **155** for another Weighty Matters or to **303** for a TOUGH puzzle.

335

Speedy Word Problems I

Answer these problems as quickly as you can. You'll have to get them all correct to score any points.

Start the clock!

Three times twelve minus five =

Seven times three plus fifteen minus four =

One hundred and five minus twenty-eight =

Seventy-eight plus one hundred and fourteen =

Seven plus ninety-five times three =

Fifty-three times eighteen =

Seventeen plus thirty-four minus five times eight =

Nine times ninety-three plus twenty-seven =

Thirty-eight plus one hundred and seventeen minus twelve =

One hundred and fifteen times three =

When you have written down the answers and recorded your time, turn to **85**.

336

Answer to 16:

The answer is 6 am again. After all, what difference does the speed of light make to the answer? It's irrelevant—only the speed of the rotation of the Earth matters here. After you've scored this puzzle, turn to **56**.

337

Answers to 273:

41 + 38 = 79	21 − 15 = 6
7 x 7 = 49	18 + 19 = 37
31 − 18 = 13	78 + 31 = 109
9 x 13 = 117	78 + 234 = 312
27 x 11 = 297	143 − 65 = 78
365 + 153 = 518	972 − 489 = 483
4,852 − 632 = 4,220	942 + 2,732 = 3,674
382 x 3 = 1,146	99 x 33 = 3,267

When you've finished scoring, turn to **372**.

338

Answer to 56:

This is one solution. You might have come to the same result slightly differently, but that's OK. Score yourself normally.

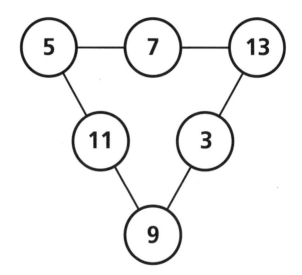

When you've finished scoring, turn to **233**.

339

The Dark Tower

An apprentice Dark Lord, having recently conquered part of the world, is slowly covering it with an evil miasma and converting it to his dark and evil ways. Now it's time for him to build his Dark Tower, from where he can rule his kingdom with an iron hand, and plot the overthrow of the goody-two-shoes elves, crush little hobbits, kidnap little girls' dolls, etc., as all evil overlords wish to. Trouble is, he's having problems working out who gets paid what.

Start the clock!

He's going to have to pay:

850 gold pieces to the Dragon Guardian and the Hell-hound Wrangler

1,300 gold pieces to the Hell-hound Wrangler and the Magician Architect

1,000 gold pieces to the Magician Architect and the Orc Overseer

1,900 gold pieces to the Orc Overseer and the Master of Slaves

3,300 gold pieces to the Master of Slaves and the Conjuror of the Demon Hordes

2,500 gold pieces to the Conjuror of the Demon Hordes and the Hell-hound Wrangler

What does each one charge for his (or its) services?

When you have an answer, turn to 171.

340

Answer to 380:

3,968. Square the previous number and subtract one.

Score yourself using the TOUGH score table, then turn to **10**.

341

Can of Worms

Start the clock!

There are four cans in a cupboard containing dog food, beef stew, cat food, and cashew nuts. Each can is of identical shape and size, and unfortunately all of the cans' labels have been mixed up, so each one has one of the other labels on it. How can you find out the contents of each can by opening only *one* can?

When you have the answer, turn to **199**.

342

Answer to 313:

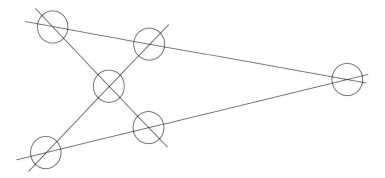

When you've finished scoring, turn to **394** for a slightly tricky puzzle.

343

Answer to 210:

HTHHTH

Score yourself using the TOUGH score table. When you're done, turn to **115**.

Only One I

Start the clock!

Only one of these objects appears in both drawings.
Can you find it?

When you think you have the answer, turn to **301**.

Answer to 179:

The key.

When you've scored your points, turn to **406**.

346

Answer to 251:

C. All the symbols have one line, one square and one circle, except for C which has two lines.

When you've scored your points, turn to **419** for a regular puzzle or to **304** for a TOUGH puzzle.

347

Write down on a piece of paper as many of the words from 408 as you can remember. You have two minutes to do this. When the time is up, turn to **415**.

348

Answer to 180:

Four beards. Remember, each King card has two faces on it, a top and bottom one.

When you've finished scoring, turn to **295**.

349

Chop Chop

Start the clock!

How long will it take to chop a wooden pole into twelve equal pieces if every cut takes a minute?

When you think you have the answer, or the time is up, turn to **51**.

350

Dracula's Combination

Start the clock!

Count Dracula has trouble remembering all the numbers he needs in the modern world, what with PIN numbers, account numbers, security numbers, insurance numbers and so on. After all, he is over 450 years old, and his memory is fading! To remember the four-figure combination of his safe, he uses his birth date: 12/28/1632.

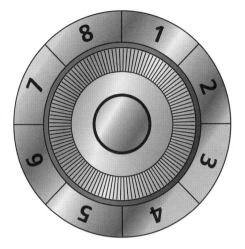

What is the combination?

When you think you have the answer, turn to **268**.

351

Answer to 211:

The match!

When you've finished scoring, turn to **226**.

Answer to 248:

Score yourself using the TOUGH score table. Now turn to **178**.

Answers to 220:

Red Herring, Green with Envy, Blue Murder, White Knight, Pink Champagne, Yellow Fever, Purple Prose, Black Ball.

They were pretty easy. Here's some that are a bit harder. Turn to **230**.

354

Answer to 420:

D. It's the musical scale: Doh, Ray, Me, Fah, Soh, Lah, Te, Doh.

Score yourself using the TOUGH score table, then turn to **120**.

355

Answer to 14:

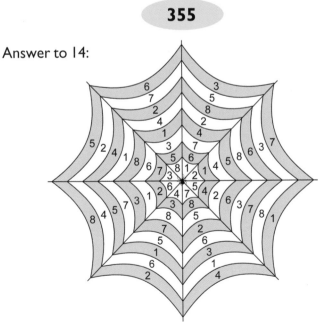

Score yourself normally. Now turn to **178**.

356

Write down on a piece of paper as many of the words from 193 as you can remember. You have two minutes to do this. When the time is up, turn to **401**.

357

How Much?

Start the clock!

The local supermarket is trying to shift some of its old stock.

A tin of beans and a tin of tuna costs $4.

A tin of beans and a tin of corned beef costs $3.20.

A tin of corned beef and a tin of tuna costs $2.40.

How much is each individual tin?

When you think you have the answers, turn to **329**.

358

Handbags at Dawn

Start the clock!

Hilary Yellow, Jane Red and Lucy Gray each have a gray handbag, a yellow handbag and a red handbag, but none of them has a handbag color that matches their name. They met unexpectedly one day.

The lady with the red handbag commented, "How odd!" to which Lucy Gray replied: "Most odd indeed!"

What color is each lady's handbag?

When you have an answer, turn to **276**.

The Race

Start the clock!

From somewhere Mike found extra reserves of energy and overtook the leader with a snarl. Seconds later he hurtled past the finish line first, with a meter or two to spare. Though the prize for the 100 meter sprint was ten grand and a fine Championship Cup, Mike didn't get either. Why?

When you think you have an answer, turn to **88**.

360

True or False? II

Start the clock!

Answer all four of these as fast as you can.

1: If all Voibles are Varbles and no Varbles are Vibbles, then no Vibbles are definitely Voibles.

2: If some Clugs are Cligs and all Clags are Cligs, then some Clugs are definitely Clags.

3: If some Nabobs are Nobabs and some Nibebs are Nebubs, then some Nabobs are definitely Nebubs.

4: If all Trimps are Tromps and all Tromps are Trumps, then all Trimps are definitely Trumps.

When you think you've got the answers (and have written them down), turn to **76**. Remember, you need to get them all correct to score any points.

Speedy Math IV

Do this math as quickly as you can and write the answers down.

Start the clock!

875 + 345 =	842 x 17 =
51 x 51 =	567 – 414 =
6,434 – 2,543 =	64,313 + 53,421 =
19 x 18=	14 x 37=
11 x 738 =	78,492 – 3,521 =
3,745 + 5,468 =	864 – 389 =
6,548 – 2,989 =	913 x 9 =
267 x 13 =	

When you're done, record the time it took you, and turn to **34** for the answers.

362

Answer to 99:

No. The tangles aren't closed and so would fall free without becoming a knot.

When you have scored yourself, turn to **293** for a slightly tricky puzzle.

Number Series II

Start the clock!

What is the next number in the series?

4, 22, 7, 19, 10, 16, 13, 13, 16, 10, ?

When you think you have the answer, turn to **43**.

Lone Wolf I

Start the clock!

Which object appears once only?

When you've got an answer, turn to **322**.

365

Answer to 84:

The box labeled B.

When you've scored your points, turn to **339**.

366

CryptoMath I

Work out what numbers each asterisk represents. Only the numbers 1 through 9 are used, and no number is used twice (including the answer).

Start the clock!

** + ** + = **, then add * = 57

When you think you've solved it, turn to **44**.

Brain fact: The heaviest brain we know of is that of the sperm whale, coming in at a massive 7,800 grams! And an elephant's brain is over three times bigger than man's, weighing in at around 4,700 grams. Though some of you playing this book might feel your brain is rather lightweight, you can take comfort in the fact that no matter how hard the puzzles seem to you, your brain must surely be heavier than a goldfish's, at 0.097 grams, or a viper's, at 0.1 grams. Surely!

Speedy Word Problems III

Answer these problems as quickly as you can.

Start the clock!

Ninety thousand four hundred and forty-three plus eighteen hundred and seventeen times three hundred and twenty-two =

One million three hundred and twenty-seven thousand plus two million four hundred thousand and eighteen =

Two hundred and fifty-five thousand and seventeen minus sixty-seven thousand and twenty-two plus one hundred and eighteen thousand =

Two hundred and twelve thousand five hundred and eighty-two plus nine thousand three hundred and four minus one hundred and four thousand three hundred and eight =

Two million nine hundred thousand nine hundred and ninety-two plus one hundred and ninety-five thousand and nineteen minus four hundred and eighty-two thousand one hundred and five =

When you've got your answers, write them down and turn to **122**.

368

Number Series I

Start the clock!

What is the next number in the series?

1, 3, 7, 15, 31, 63, ?

When you think you have the answer, turn to **149**.

369

Answer to 317:

99 + (9 ÷ 9) = 100. Fiendish, eh!

After you have finished scoring, turn to **407**.

370

Answer to 156:

2 x 40 + 5 + 1 = 86, then add 7 = 93

You might have been able to come up with a different solution than the one given here. If so, that's fine, score yourself normally. Score yourself using the TOUGH score table, then turn to **238**.

When Number Series Go Wrong I

Which one of these numbers doesn't belong in the series?

Example—if the series was 2, 4, 6, 8, 10, 13, then 13 would be wrong as it's a simple n + 2 number series.

So let's try a real one.

Start the clock!

9, 7, 4, 6, 3, 5, 2, 4, 1, 3

When you think you have the answer, turn to **242**.

372

Shapes and Codes I

Start the clock!

Have a careful look at the shapes and codes below. Which code matches the shape at the end of the row?

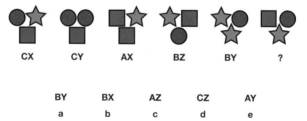

When you think you have the answer or time runs out, turn to **36**.

373

Answer to 109:

Five birds and nine bees (bees have six legs!). When you've finished scoring, turn to **253** for another Birds and Bees conundrum, or to **341** for a TOUGH puzzle.

374

Missing Number III

Start the clock!

What's the missing number?

8	5	11
6	17	1
10	2	?

When you have finished scoring, turn to **38**.

375

Answer to 206:

45 stubs will make 9 candles. Once you've used those you'll have 9 stubs from which you can make 1 additional full candle, so that's 10 full candles in total, or 5 hours of light.

When you've finished scoring turn to **292**.

376

Foot and Mouth

Start the clock!

A farmer has a herd of 102 cows, made up of Jersey and Guernsey cows. Unfortunately, foot and mouth has broken out on his farm—$1/13$ of the Jersey cows and $1/19$ of the Guernsey cows have caught the disease. How many Jersey cows are there, and how many Guernsey cows are there?

When you're ready, or if you run out of time, turn to **167**.

377

Nautical Ladders

Start the clock!

A ship is moored at the docks. A ladder with rungs a foot apart is hung over the side, with twelve rungs showing from the deck to the sea. If the tide rises at the rate of half a foot an hour, how much of the ladder will still be above water after four hours?

When you think you have the answer, or the time is up, turn to **124**.

378

Answer to 239:

There were 23 assassins.

When you've finished scoring, turn to **6** for a TOUGH puzzle.

379

Speed Test

Start the clock!

A biker takes his Harley Davidson in for a tune-up. On the way to the auto shop he manages a speed of 60 miles per hour. On the way back, his new souped-up Harley does 90 miles per hour. He travels the same distance each way—but what is the average speed of his entire journey?

When you're ready with an answer, turn to **261**.

 380

Number Series III

Start the clock!

What's the next number in the series?

2, 3, 8, 63, ?

When you think you have the answer, turn to **340**.

381

Answer to 255:

There are 4 sisters and 3 brothers. Julie has 3 sisters and 3 brothers, and Pete has 2 brothers and 4 sisters.

When you've finished scoring, turn to **177** for the next puzzle.

382

Answer to 332:

50 divided by a half actually equals 100. So the correct answer is 105.

When you've finished scoring, turn to **109**.

383

Answer to 397:

The missing number is 1. The two numbers on the left and on the right of every row are counted as a single number. From the right-hand number, the left-hand number is subtracted to give the middle number. So, 54 – 45 = 9, 27 – 22 = 5, and 47 – 46 = 1.

Score yourself using the TOUGH score table, then turn to **31**.

384

Write down on a piece of paper as many of the things from 235 as you can remember. You have two minutes to do this. When the time is up, turn to **223**.

385

Sheep I

Start the clock!

Imagine a sheep pen. Inside are a bunch of sheep. Some of them are ewes. The number of sheep heads multiplied by the number of sheep hooves multiplied by the number of ewes' tongues equals 200. How many sheep are there, and how many of them are ewes?

When you're ready, turn to **196** for the answer.

386

Rapunzel

Start the clock!

A fair maiden has been locked in a tall tower by an evil knight, but her golden hair is magical and she can grow it at will—long enough for her champion to climb up and rescue her. When she casts her spell, her hair will grow by half its initial length in the first second, then by a third of its new length in the next second, then by a quarter of its length in the following second, and so on. Now, given that her hair is one meter long to start with and the tower is fifty meters high, the question you have to ask yourself is when or if her hair will reach the ground.

When you think you have the answer, or when the time runs out, turn to **137**. Not far to go now!

387

Answers to 228:

B and F are the same.

When you've finished scoring, turn to **225** for another regular Mondrian puzzle, or to **236** for a TOUGH Mondrian puzzle.

Speedy Unpleasant Divisions III

Answer these problems as quickly as you can. Note that you'll need to get them all correct to score any points.

Start the clock!

8 ÷ 4 =	21 ÷ 7 =
54 ÷ 9 =	702 ÷ 13 =
112 ÷ 8 =	186 ÷ 31 =
126 ÷ 18 =	1,242 ÷ 23 =

When you're done, turn to **264** for the answers.

Answers to 234:

1: Nephew—the "opposite" of niece.
2: Cannon—the only one that unequivocally fires a shell.
3: Uncle.
4: Marmalade—both wine and marmalade require a chemical reaction to occur.
5: Hatbox—hand fits in glove, hat fits in hatbox (and not in a head!).

6: Nut.

7: Brush.

When you have finished scoring, turn to **243** for a regular puzzle, and to **153** for a TOUGH puzzle.

390

Odd Sums

Start the clock!

Draw two lines across this number grid, dividing the numbers in such a way that the lines cut the grid into a number of pieces. The numbers in each piece must add up to the same odd number.

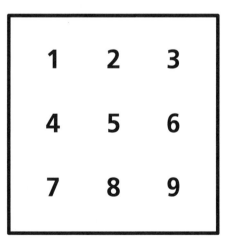

When you think you have the answer, or if time runs out, turn to **9**.

391

Answer to 161:

60. Find the square root of each top number and add them together. Then add together the two bottom numbers. Then multiply the two remaining numbers together to get your answer.

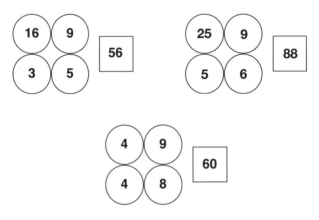

Score yourself using the TOUGH score table, then turn to **422**.

392

Answer to 316:

45. The series increases by an increasing number each time—i. e., by 6, then 8, then 10, then 12.

When you've scored yourself, turn to **234**.

393

Egg On Your Face

Start the clock!

Which of these two sentences is correct: "The yolk of the egg are white" or "The yolk of the egg is white?" When you think you have the answer or the time is up, turn to **140**.

394

Start the clock!

Two soldiers were sitting in the barracks, a Colonel and a Private. The Private was the son of the Colonel, but the Colonel was not the father of the Private. How is this possible?

When you think you have an answer, turn to **7**.

395

Answer to 275:

It could be written as 23:45 6/7/89 or 23456789.

When you've finished scoring, turn to **231**.

396

Triangles and Squares

Start the clock!

How many triangles and squares are there in this diagram?

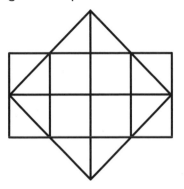

When you think you have an answer, turn to **176**.

397

Missing Number IV

Start the clock!

What's the missing number?

4	5	9	5	4
2	2	5	2	7
4	6	?	4	7

When you think you have the answer, or the time has run out, turn to **383**.

398

Answer to 416:

F. They're the five permanent members of the United Nations Security Council: United States, Britain, Russia, China and France.

Score yourself using the TOUGH score table, then turn to **288**.

Heads in Your Head II

Remember, you're not allowed to use real coins!

Start the clock!

Imagine six coins in a row, all heads up.

Now turn over both coins on the outer edges.

Now exchange them with the coins next to them.

Now move the two innermost coins to the outside and turn them over.

Now take the coin next to the one on the left-hand end, and move it out to the left-hand end and turn it over.

Now take the coin next to the one on the right-hand end, and move it out to the right-hand end and turn it over.

What have you left?

When you think you have the answer, turn to **72**.

400

Answer to 417:

Nine, seven feet of wood plus his own two feet!

When you've finished scoring, turn to **59**.

401

Answers to 193:

Here are the words again:

Pastel	Idea	Feeble	Glaze
Probable	Sometimes	Never	Team
Humor	Chosen	Deep	Consular
Theology	Wednesday	However	Deplore
Ascend	Conclusion	Innovate	Side

Score yourself *one* point for every word you got right.

When you are ready, turn to **317**.

402

Answer to 146:

There were fifteen men in the King's bodyguard.

Score yourself using the TOUGH scoring table, then turn to **6** for a TOUGH puzzle.

403

Answers to 226:

Blueberry Pie, the Black Sea, Red in the Face, Gray around the Gills, Blue-eyed Boy, Brownie Points, White Noise, Between the Devil and the Deep Blue Sea.

When you've finished scoring, turn to **104**.

404

Answer to 181:

V (for violet). The series uses the first letters of the colors of the rainbow.

When you've finished scoring, turn to **3**.

405

Answer to 327:

Hobbit City is 113 miles away—each letter corresponds to its position in the alphabet. So an A is 1 mile, an E is 5 miles; Z is 26 miles and so on.

Score yourself using the TOUGH score table, then turn to **22**.

406

Jumbled Equation II

The following equations have had their numbers jumbled. Rearrange them so they make sense. Mathematical signs remain where they are.

Start the clock!

$$8 \times 4 = 2$$

$$21 \times 3 = 4$$

$$5 \times 4 = 80$$

$$31 \times 6 = 84$$

When you think you have answers, turn to **106**.

407

Dark Lord's Bonus Scheme

Start the clock!

A Dark Lord is pleased with the service provided by some of his Orcish captains, evil monsters and minions. He decides to give out some of his hard-won gold as a reward.

To his favorite Guardian of the Gates of Doom he gives 2 gold pieces more than half of the money he has in his Strongbox. To his best Orc Captain, Agrash the Bonecrusher and Dispenser of General Mayhem, he gives 4 gold pieces more than half of the remainder. To his sniveling, groveling and wonderfully sycophantic minion, Bogle, he gives 4 gold pieces more than half of the remainder. He is now left with 4 gold pieces. Consequently, his mood suddenly darkens and he executes them all instantly, just to get his gold back. However, that's another story—how much gold did he start with in his Strongbox?

When you think you have an answer, turn to **60**.

408

Start the clock!

You have two minutes to memorize as many of these words as you can:

Plough	Plate	Spoon	Rabbit
Flesh	Shield	Mauve	Lava
Bean	Goose	Trombone	Spaghetti
Nut	Mail	Microwave	Tree
Wheel	Tweezers	Jacket	Cake

When the time is up, turn to **347**.

409

An Alchemist's Jars

Start the clock!

An Alchemist has arranged his potions and elixirs in such a way that each shelf holds a total of 9 liters, contained in three types of jar—small, medium and large. How many liters does each jar type contain?

When you think you have an answer, turn to **70**.

410

Answers to 304:

$(2 \times 4) + 7 = 15$

$(4 \times 3) + 7 = 19$

$(6 \times 14) + 8 = 92$

You may be able to get viable answers with different combinations. If so, that's fine, score yourself normally. Score yourself using the TOUGH score table, then turn to **299**.

411

Answers to 286:

$3 \times 9 = 27$

$8 \times 8 = 64$

$7 \times 6 = 42$

You might be able to get equally valid results with other combinations. If so, that's fine, score yourself normally. When you've finished scoring, turn to **120**.

412

Answer for 47:

Six years.

When you've finished scoring, turn to **18**.

413

Answer to 96:

Anywhere! During those times of the season when the days are growing shorter, wherever you are on the globe, you'll see the sunrise twice in a 24-hour period.

When you've finished scoring, turn to **288**.

414

Answers to 71:

$12 \div 4 = 3$

$72 \div 9 = 8$

$117 \div 9 = 13$

$114 \div 19 = 6$

$28 \div 7 = 4$

$1,365 \div 21 = 65$

$280 \div 35 = 8$

$1,736 \div 56 = 31$

Score yourself using the TOUGH score table, then turn to **59**.

415

Answers to 2:

Here are the words again:

Plough	Plate	Spoon	Rabbit
Flesh	Shield	Mauve	Lava
Bean	Goose	Trombone	Spaghetti
Nut	Mail	Microwave	Tree
Wheel	Tweezers	Jacket	Cake

Score yourself half a point for every word you got right. Then turn to **202** for a regular puzzle, or to **191** for a TOUGH memory puzzle.

416

What's Next? 1

Start the clock!

You'll need to have a united sense of security to get this one! What's next in the series?

U, B, R, C, ?

When you have the answer, turn to **398**.

417

Feet

Start the clock!

A lumberjack keeps his timber in a shed. He has fourteen feet of timber in the shed. One day, he enters the shed, takes seven feet worth of timber and leaves.

How many feet does he leave with?

When you have the answer, turn to **400**.

418

Answer to 266:

Daughter or niece.

When you've finished scoring, turn to **94**.

419

Jumbled Equation I

The following equations have had their numbers jumbled. Rearrange them so they make sense. Mathematical signs remain where they are.

Start the clock!

$$68 + 14 = 31$$

$$7 \times 2 = 39$$

$$41 \times 4 = 14$$

When you think you have answers, turn to **97**.

What's Next? II

Start the clock!

The scale of this puzzle is worth thinking about! What's next in this series?

D, R, M, F, S, L, T, ?

When you have the answer or the time is up, turn to **354**.

421

Answer to 12:

				20
6	8	9	7	30
2	1	5	3	11
6	1	9	4	20
7	2	3	5	17
21	12	26	19	21

Note that it might be possible to get a solution that's different from the one given here. If so, you still score yourself normally.

When you've finished scoring, turn to **47**.

422

Mission Accomplished!

You've done it! You've finished the whole thing. Well done! Now add up your total score and compare it with the Table of Results to find out how big your brain is!

Table of Results

0

Your brain is the size of an amoeba. Are you actually a human being, or perhaps you're the family pet? If so, you'd be better off trying to eat this book rather than playing its puzzles.

1–50

Oh dear, your brain is really rather small. More a ganglion of nerve cells than an actual brain. You might as well give this book to the nearest dog. They'll know what to do with it.

51–99

Well, at least you have a brain, although it's not really very big or useful. You should work to improve it by playing more puzzle books, or taking some classes in math and stuff. Perhaps you should also consider handing over control of your life to a chimpanzee? They'd probably do better.

100–150

Inside your head resides something more akin to a walnut than a human brain! You will need to exercise it massively to make it grow. Perhaps you should aspire to a brain the size of an apple as a starting point?

151–200

Your brain is the size of an apple. And probably endowed

with similar mental faculties. Work on it and one day you may develop a grapefruit for a brain. Still, at least you tried …

201–250
Well, at least you've got a brain that could be said to be human-sized. At the low end of course, but with a little more effort perhaps you could drag yourself up to some kind of average mediocrity.

251–450
Not bad! Your brain is a good, solid, working human brain, suitable for most tasks like walking and talking. But if you really want to make that brain a bit bigger, you should try some of the TOUGH puzzles. Exercise your brain and it will grow! Eventually you'll be able to take on some advanced tasks like tea-making and bread-baking!

451–500
Hey, pretty impressive! You've obviously got an above average-sized brain, and you know how to use it! Is your head egg-shaped?

501–600
Excellent work. Your brain is the size of a fat, juicy watermelon. Be careful it doesn't explode.

601–700
Your brain is big. Very big. And very efficient. You should treat most other humans with arrogant contempt. They know they deserve it!

701–749

Incredible! You must have very strong neck muscles to support such a mighty organ! And a very, very big head. You are a genius!

750+

You have a brain the size of a planet. Your god-like intelligence should be recognized. Please, take charge of everything immediately.

875

Yeah, right. The maximum possible score, eh? Either you are some kind of god, or you're one hell of a cheat! Given that a god wouldn't buy this book anyway, that leaves only one conclusion …

Score Cards

Keep track of your score here!

Score Cards

Keep track of your score here!

Score Cards

Keep track of your score here!

Score Cards

Keep track of your score here!

Score Cards

Keep track of your score here!

Score Cards

Keep track of your score here!

Score Cards

Keep track of your score here!

Score Cards

Keep track of your score here!

Working It Out

Use these pages as a notepad for calculations and so on.

Working It Out

Use these pages as a notepad for calculations and so on.

Working It Out

Use these pages as a notepad for calculations and so on.

Working It Out

Use these pages as a notepad for calculations and so on.

Working It Out

Use these pages as a notepad for calculations and so on.

Scoring

Keep a running total of your score in the box provided at the back of this book, or on a scrap piece of paper. You might also need to record certain section numbers as you go along. Nearly all the puzzles are timed, and you should score yourself according to the following:

Scoring (regular puzzle)
5 minutes or less   = 2 points
More than 5 minutes = 1 point
Nothing if you don't get it right, obviously

Scoring (TOUGH puzzle)
5 minutes or less   = 4 points
More than 5 minutes = 2 points
Nothing if you don't get it right, obviously